LOUIS
ARMSTRONG

LOUIS ARMSTRONG

Sam Tanenhaus

Senior Consulting Editor
Nathan Irvin Huggins
Director
W.E.B. Du Bois Institute for Afro-American Research
Harvard University

CHELSEA HOUSE PUBLISHERS
New York   Philadelphia

Chelsea House Publishers
Editor-in-Chief Nancy Toff
Executive Editor Remmel T. Nunn
Managing Editor Karyn Gullen Browne
Copy Chief Juliann Barbato
Picture Editor Adrian G. Allen
Art Director Maria Epes
Manufacturing Manager Gerald Levine

Black Americans of Achievement
Senior Editor Richard Rennert

Staff for LOUIS ARMSTRONG
Associate Editor Perry King
Deputy Copy Chief Ellen Scordato
Editorial Assistant Susan DeRosa
Picture Researcher Linda Peer
Assistant Art Director Laurie Jewell
Design Assistant Seth Wimpfheimer
Production Coordinator Joseph Romano
Cover Illustration Alan J. Nahigian

5   7   9   8   6   4

Library of Congress Cataloging in Publication Data
Tanenhaus, Sam.
  Louis Armstrong.

  (Black Americans of Achievement)
  Bibliography: p.
  Includes index.
  Summary: A biography of the famous trumpeter who was
one of the first great improvisers in jazz history.
  1. Armstrong, Louis, 1900–1971—Juvenile literature.
2. Jazz musicians—United States—Biography—Juvenile lit-
erature. [1. Armstrong, Louis, 1900–1971. 2. Musicians. 3.
Jazz music. 4. Afro-American—Biography] I. Title. II.
Series.
ML3930.A75T3   1989   785.42'092'4 [B]
[92]   88-20208
ISBN 1-55546-571-4
      0-7910-0221-7 (pbk.)

CONTENTS

———— ✿ ————

BLACK AMERICANS OF ACHIEVEMENT

RALPH ABERNATHY
civil rights leader

MUHAMMAD ALI
heavyweight champion

RICHARD ALLEN
religious leader and social activist

LOUIS ARMSTRONG
musician

ARTHUR ASHE
tennis great

JOSEPHINE BAKER
entertainer

JAMES BALDWIN
author

BENJAMIN BANNEKER
scientist and mathematician

AMIRI BARAKA
poet and playwright

COUNT BASIE
bandleader and composer

ROMARE BEARDEN
artist

JAMES BECKWOURTH
frontiersman

MARY MCLEOD
BETHUNE
educator

BLANCHE BRUCE
politician

RALPH BUNCHE
diplomat

GEORGE WASHINGTON
CARVER
botanist

CHARLES CHESNUTT
author

BILL COSBY
entertainer

PAUL CUFFE
merchant and abolitionist

FATHER DIVINE
religious leader

FREDERICK DOUGLASS
abolitionist editor

CHARLES DREW
physician

W.E.B. DU BOIS
scholar and activist

PAUL LAURENCE DUNBAR
poet

KATHERINE DUNHAM
dancer and choreographer

MARIAN WRIGHT EDELMAN
civil rights leader and lawyer

DUKE ELLINGTON
bandleader and composer

RALPH ELLISON
author

JULIUS ERVING
basketball great

JAMES FARMER
civil rights leader

ELLA FITZGERALD
singer

MARCUS GARVEY
black-nationalist leader

DIZZY GILLESPIE
musician

PRINCE HALL
social reformer

W. C. HANDY
father of the blues

WILLIAM HASTIE
educator and politician

MATTHEW HENSON
explorer

CHESTER HIMES
author

BILLIE HOLIDAY
singer

JOHN HOPE
educator

LENA HORNE
entertainer

LANGSTON HUGHES
poet

ZORA NEALE HURSTON
author

JESSE JACKSON
civil rights leader and politician

JACK JOHNSON
heavyweight champion

JAMES WELDON JOHNSON
author

SCOTT JOPLIN
composer

BARBARA JORDAN
politician

MARTIN LUTHER KING, JR.
civil rights leader

ALAIN LOCKE
scholar and educator

JOE LOUIS
heavyweight champion

RONALD MCNAIR
astronaut

MALCOLM X
militant black leader

THURGOOD MARSHALL
Supreme Court justice

ELIJAH MUHAMMAD
religious leader

JESSE OWENS
champion athlete

CHARLIE PARKER
musician

GORDON PARKS
photographer

SIDNEY POITIER
actor

ADAM CLAYTON POWELL, JR.
political leader

LEONTYNE PRICE
opera singer

A. PHILIP RANDOLPH
labor leader

PAUL ROBESON
singer and actor

JACKIE ROBINSON
baseball great

BILL RUSSELL
basketball great

JOHN RUSSWURM
publisher

SOJOURNER TRUTH
antislavery activist

HARRIET TUBMAN
antislavery activist

NAT TURNER
slave revolt leader

DENMARK VESEY
slave revolt leader

MADAME C. J. WALKER
entrepreneur

BOOKER T. WASHINGTON
educator

HAROLD WASHINGTON
politician

WALTER WHITE
civil rights leader and author

RICHARD WRIGHT
author

ON ACHIEVEMENT

Coretta Scott King

Before you begin this book, I hope you will ask yourself what the word excellence means to you. I think that it's a question we should all ask, and keep asking as we grow older and change. Because the truest answer to it should never change. When you think of excellence, perhaps you think of success at work; or of becoming wealthy; or meeting the right person, getting married, and having a good family life.

Those important goals are worth striving for, but there is a better way to look at excellence. As Martin Luther King, Jr., said in one of his last sermons, "I want you to be first in love. I want you to be first in moral excellence. I want you to be first in generosity. If you want to be important, wonderful. If you want to be great, wonderful. But recognize that he who is greatest among you shall be your servant."

My husband, Martin Luther King, Jr., knew that the true meaning of achievement is service. When I met him, in 1952, he was already ordained as a Baptist preacher and was working towards a doctoral degree at Boston University. I was studying at the New England Conservatory and dreamed of accomplishments in music. We married a year later, and after I graduated the following year we moved to Montgomery, Alabama. We didn't know it then, but our notions of achievement were about to undergo a dramatic change.

You may have read or heard about what happened next. What began with the boycott of a local bus line grew into a national movement, and by the time he was assassinated in 1968 my husband had fashioned a black movement powerful enough to shatter forever the practice of racial segregation. What you may not have read about is where he got his method for resisting injustice without compromising his religious beliefs.

He got the strategy of nonviolence from a man of a different race, who lived in a distant country, and even practiced a different religion. The man was Mahatma Gandhi, the great leader of India, who devoted his life to serving humanity in the spirit of love and nonviolence. It was in these principles that Martin discovered his method for social reform. More than anything else, those two principles were the key to his achievements.

This book is about black Americans who served society through the excellence of their achievements. It forms a part of the rich history of black men and women in America—a history of stunning accomplishments in every field of human endeavor, from literature and art to science, industry, education, diplomacy, athletics, jurisprudence, even polar exploration.

Not all of the people in this history had the same ideals, but I think you will find something that all of them have in common. Like Martin Luther King, Jr., they all decided to become "drum majors" and serve humanity. In that principle—whether it was expressed in books, inventions, or song—they found something outside themselves to use as a goal and a guide. Something that showed them a way to serve others, instead of living only for themselves.

Reading the stories of these courageous men and women not only helps us discover the principles that we will use to guide our own lives, but it teaches us about our black heritage and about America itself. It is crucial for us to know the heroes and heroines of our history and to realize that the price we paid in our struggle for equality in America was dear. But we must also understand that we have gotten as far as we have partly because America's democratic system and ideals made it possible.

We still are struggling with racism and prejudice. But the great men and women in this series are a tribute to the spirit of our democratic ideals and the system in which they have flourished. And that makes their stories special, and worth knowing. ❧

LOUIS
ARMSTRONG

1

"WEST END BLUES"

ON THE MORNING of June 28, 1928, six of the slickest jazzmen in Chicago, Illinois, trudged into a recording studio shortly after finishing a grueling session in a late-night club. One by one, they slumped onto hard wooden chairs and caught their breath. Then they unpacked their instruments.

Zutty Singleton pulled out drumsticks and a woodblock and placed a cymbal on a small stand. Mancy Cara adjusted the tuning pegs on his banjo. Jimmy Strong slipped a reed into his clarinet. Fred Robinson breathed into his trombone, testing out the volume of its low tones. Earl "Fatha" Hines seated himself at the studio's grand piano and teased liquid melodies out of its keyboard. And the group's leader, 29-year-old Louis Armstrong, fished in his suit coat for a metal mouthpiece that he attached to his trumpet. Then he blew a series of quicksilver notes, lightly fingering the instrument's three valves.

All six musicians were members of a large dance band that played in nightclubs and dance halls several nights a week. In their spare time, they formed smaller combos such as this one and made records. They did not receive royalties on sales of the disks, but they gladly accepted the flat fee that the studio work brought

The world of jazz was forever changed in 1925, when Armstrong teamed up with (from left to right) Johnny St. Cyr, Johnny Dodds, Kid Ory, and Lil Hardin to form an innovative group called the Hot Five. Armstrong, the band's featured performer, was the only original member of the Hot Five to play on "West End Blues," recorded three years later.

Dixieland grew out of the marching music played by New Orleans bands such as this one, photographed about 1910. Later Dixieland groups dispensed with the tuba and added a banjo to accentuate the rhythm.

them. Each session paid about $50 per man, although Armstrong, a rising star in the music world, earned two or three times as much.

The music they played was known as "Chicago-style" jazz, a refinement of "Dixieland," dance music that was invented in the early 1900s in New Orleans, Louisiana. Upbeat and highly rhythmic, Dixieland called for several instruments to play at once and at breakneck speed, weaving a dense tapestry of nonstop sound. The only interruption came during solo "breaks," in which an individual bandsman handled the melody himself and then yielded to the next man.

Since 1925, Armstrong had been reshaping Dixieland into a more sophisticated musical form, especially with the small ensembles he led in the studio, collectively known as the Hot Five. He quieted Dixieland's chaotic din, spotlighted individual instruments, and, most important, he urged his sidemen to expand their solos beyond the bounds of the prescribed tune. On his most successful numbers—

"Muskrat Ramble," "Struttin' with Some Barbecue," and others—he treated the given melody as a kind of rough draft and improvised the final product on the spot.

Eventually, most jazz would be performed in this way; but in the 1920s, few artists met the demands of spontaneous creation. Armstrong, however, had already mastered this new method of playing. Compared to most soloists, who were content merely to embroider the melodies they performed, he seemed a sorcerer, capable of transforming drab tunes into sparkling musical statements.

Many other players were thrilled by what Armstrong was doing, but few grasped how he did it. He himself was not exactly sure. Like most artists, he simply followed his instincts, playing the music in a way that sounded right to him. He was astonished when other trumpeters started copying him.

As splendidly as he improvised, Armstrong had yet to make improvisation itself the focus of a recording. However, on this June day in 1928, he had selected a tune that held unusual promise. It was called "West End Blues" and it was so straightforward—so workmanlike and familiar sounding—that it offered a rare test of his solo skills.

Earlier in the week, Armstrong had rehearsed in his apartment with Hines, who was also a gifted improviser, and they had lit upon several ingenious twists that might result in an exciting dialogue between their two instruments. In keeping with Armstrong's method, they had left some rough spots unsmoothed, confident that inspiration would strike them during the recording. Once the session began, Armstrong was prepared to run through "West End Blues" several times or more—however long it took him and his sidemen to achieve the right result.

Everyone was prepared for a grueling session—not only because of Armstrong's exacting standards but also because in the 1920s recording techniques

"Heebie Jeebies," Armstrong's first hit record, introduced listeners to scat. He reportedly improvised his "vocal chorus" of nonsense words after he accidentally dropped his lyric sheet.

were still primitive. A single mistake—a fluffed note, a missed beat—meant doing the entire piece over, from beginning to end. Armstrong hoped he and his musicians could make several errorless recordings, then choose the one that sounded best. It was important that all six players be primed to perform well, but it was also essential that they be relaxed, unafraid to take risks that might lead to a memorable record.

Armstrong, who had dozens of recordings and a few hits under his belt, put the men at ease with lighthearted banter, his mouth widening into a grin so inviting it had long ago earned him the nickname "Dippermouth." Humor came naturally to him. It was his trademark at the Vendome Theatre and the Sunset Cafe, where Chicago audiences delighted not only in his stirring solos but also in the warm rasp of his vocals and the broad comedy of his stage act. And Armstrong's first hit record, "Heebie Jeebies," released in 1926, had caused a national sensation because of a witty innovation, called "scat," in which he replaced the tune's rather dull lyrics with outrageous nonsense syllables ad-libbed in the studio.

But there was no place for jokes on "West End Blues." It was a slow, mournful tune, reminiscent of a funeral dirge. Even though it had no lyrics, it spoke plainly of loss and disappointment. Armstrong knew he had to evoke the tragic meaning of "West End Blues" rather than make it the mere vehicle for flashy play.

While keeping this in mind, Armstrong was also aware of the limitations of the OKeh Phonograph Corporation's recording studio. A barely furnished room, it bore little resemblance to the places where records are made today. It did not have any sound booths, electronic boards covered with levers and knobs, or electrical cords crossing the floor in knotted tangles.

There was not even a microphone. Musicians at OKeh—and any other studio in the late 1920s—

made a record by crowding around a crude contraption topped with a wide-mouthed metal horn. The notes they played funneled down its tapered shaft and into a vibrating needle that etched markings onto a wax cylinder. Later, this cylinder would be detached from the wooden frame and pressed against thick vinyl disks, producing records.

After his musicians had warmed up, Armstrong lifted his trumpet, fingered its valves, tapped out or spoke the beat ("One, two, three, four"), then signaled to the others and to the lone recording engineer that he was about to start. The group sailed along nicely until the cymbal fell off Zutty Singleton's drum and clanged to the floor. Today, such a mishap would not mar the recording. The band would finish the cut, Singleton would lay down a separate track on tape, and a studio technician would splice it in with the other instruments. But not in 1928. The whole band would have to try again.

Like the musicians in this New York City recording studio in the early 1920s, Armstrong's Hot Five combo aimed their instruments at a single horn that filtered the sounds onto a wax cylinder. Any mistakes made while recording could not be corrected.

On the second take, Singleton blundered once more, this time mistiming his entrance on the last part of the song. His colleagues did not mind. The first two cuts had been full of excellent playing, and they felt confident that the next take would be even better.

For the third time, Armstrong signaled he was ready. As before, he blazed into a long introductory solo, speeding up and down the musical scale, his tone rich, warm, and golden. Each note sprang out of his trumpet like a fresh thought before another leaped up to take its place. When we listen to this opening solo today, we are so astonished by Armstrong's artistry—by the enameled brightness of his style—that we scarcely notice how far he has strayed from traditional blues.

Armstrong reminds us soon enough, however, by suddenly veering into a muted rendition of the main melody, serving up the blues in the deliberate manner we expect. But instead of returning us to recognizable ground, this shift adds to our confusion. The contrast with the fiery introduction is so pronounced that we feel nervous, as when a jubilant person abruptly turns to us with a pained look.

Before we can adjust, Armstrong foils us again by capping this second solo with a series of notes that dance up the scale like a sprightly bugle call. We now realize that "West End Blues" promises to trick us at every turn. Joy has already collapsed into sadness, and sadness blossomed into joy. It will be pointless to outguess Armstrong. We will be lucky even to keep up with him.

We momentarily get our bearings when the other instruments join in, restating the main melody. Next come two spare solos—one on trombone, the other on clarinet—both backed by the steady *clop* of Singleton's woodblock. The mood is now wistful, sad but with a pleasant tang, like a dusky afternoon in October. Armstrong heightens this mood when he

Earl "Fatha" Hines, a pianist whose personal elegance matched his smooth solos, joined Armstrong's Hot Five in 1928. He is shown here 10 years later, after he became a successful bandleader.

reenters—not with his trumpet but as a vocalist, singing scat. He begins a silken dialogue with Jimmy Strong's clarinet, trading identical notes that resemble soft sighs.

It is now Earl Hines's turn. Another surprise: He disrupts the calm interlude of Armstrong's vocals by swinging into a frisky piano solo laced with elegant frills. The change is jarring. As beautifully as Hines plays, there is something offensive about the rippling shimmer of his notes; they seem to ignore the sadness in Armstrong's vocals. Armstrong himself has thus far shown how sorrow and joy can be stitched into a seamless whole. Hines implies that these two emotions must remain at odds. His sly solo does not simply repudiate Armstrong; it dares him to take a stand.

Armstrong seems to have two choices. He can either revert to the exuberant joy of his flashy opening solo or reinforce the sadness of the main melody. He does neither—or, rather, he combines both emotions into one of defiant rage, launching a single long note that arcs heedlessly above the chords pounded steadily by the piano and echoed by the other instruments. It is as if Armstrong intends to take them all on, like a man squaring off against a mob. His single note surges ahead, his sidemen plow on—and we grow increasingly tense, asking ourselves, How long can this continue?

At last relief comes. Armstrong releases the single note and then looses a stunning flurry of rapid phrases, each jolting us with its ferocity and precision. The onslaught buries the other instruments, which fade into a quiet drone. Moments pass before the piano returns, meekly this time. It joins the trumpet in a kind of truce, and Armstrong ends the duel with three forgiving notes.

After the piece was finished, a pensive silence settled over the musicians. Then they erupted ecstatically. They felt as excited as explorers sighting a new continent. Armstrong had made many recordings before—some of them classics—but never one like this. Weeks later, when the record was issued, he and Hines listened to it over and over—10, 15, 20 times.

So did jazz musicians throughout America. They sensed that Armstrong had taken the Chicago sound to a new plateau and that all soloists must now rethink their approach to playing. No longer would deft professionalism suffice. As soloists, they would have to find something to say, disclosing recesses of feeling hidden even from themselves. The 3 minutes and 16 seconds of "West End Blues" gave birth to a kind of musical storytelling. And Armstrong had discovered the key for telling such a story: improvisation.

Today, improvisation is synonymous with jazz. In most modern pieces, the passages played by the whole band serve mainly to introduce a sequence of long solos invented on the spot by remarkably adept and highly trained musicians. These solos are not indulgences. Each player must work carefully within the chords of the tune that the band is playing and within a specified time frame. And at every moment, each musician must be aware of what the others are up to. A good improviser, like a good conversationalist, listens as well as he speaks.

Armstrong was the first great improviser in jazz history—possibly the greatest ever. What impressed almost everyone who heard him was not only the notes he chose to play but also his ability to speak through his instrument. Even on his first scratchy recordings, made when he was only a sideman, a special quality shone through his playing that set it apart.

Armstrong proved that jazz was not just entertainment but a highly sophisticated form of art, and that a great jazz player could communicate through his instrument rather than merely play it. It was an achievement that would lead him to Broadway and Hollywood. It would make him the most famous and beloved musician in the world and bring him face to face with presidents and kings.

No one can explain why this gift was bestowed on Armstrong and not someone else, although there are several reasons why he—and not some other soloist—changed the direction of popular music. Talent, of course, was one reason for his success. Another was his character. Still another reason was New Orleans, the extraordinary delta city that gave birth to jazz—and also to Louis Armstrong, in a ghetto known as "the Battlefield." ◄◘►

Armstrong in 1928, at about the time he recorded "West End Blues." He subsequently rose to stardom and became one of the most photographed and widely recognized people in the world.

2

RAW BEGINNINGS

LEGEND HAS IT that Louis Armstrong was born on July 4, 1900, but no document records this date. Indeed, the available evidence suggests he was probably born a year or two earlier, most likely in 1899. In any case, the circumstances of his birth were highly unpromising.

Louis's father, Willie Armstrong, was born in New Orleans in the 1870s and remained there all his life. For more than 30 years, he shoveled coal into boilers at a small turpentine plant in the city's black ghetto. He stayed with the company long enough to become a supervisor—a considerable achievement for a black man in a time and place that elevated few blacks to positions of responsibility.

Willie Armstrong stood out in other ways, too. According to his son Louis, he was a "real sharp man, tall and handsome and well built [who] made the chicks swoon." One of his conquests was Mary Ann (better known as Mayann) Miles, a country girl from Boutte, a whistle-stop outside New Orleans. She ventured to the city as a young girl, and while still in her teens she met and wed Willie, who abandoned her immediately after the birth of Louis, their first child. Willie Armstrong subsequently contributed nothing to the family's welfare, leaving them to struggle alone.

Houses in New Orleans' vieux carré—the old quarter of Armstrong's hometown. Founded by French explorers in 1718 and governed by France and Spain through the 18th century, the city still retains a European flavor.

A turn-of-the-century view of Basin Street in the heart of White Storyville, the wealthier half of the district in which Armstrong was raised. The turreted building in the foreground is Lulu White's Mahogany Hall, the swankiest brothel in the city.

Forced to become a breadwinner, Mayann Armstrong had few job options. She left Louis with his paternal grandmother, Josephine Armstrong, moved around the corner to Perdido Street, and was employed on and off as a maid. She also worked as a prostitute, a common occupation among poor black women in New Orleans and one she had possibly pursued before—and even during—her marriage.

There is no doubt that Louis's mother prized male companionship. A short, stubby woman, she had energy and flair and attracted at least six different replacements after her husband deserted her. These "stepfathers" drifted in and out of the household, as did Willie Armstrong, who stayed long enough to father a second child, Beatrice, born two years after Louis. A short time after his sister was born, Louis resumed living with his mother on Perdido Street.

Even with two children to care for, Mayann Armstrong continued her carefree habits, sometimes disappearing from their home on sprees that lasted for days. On those occasions, Louis was again cared for by his grandmother Josephine. She was a disciplinarian who packed her grandson off to school and church and swatted his rump with a branch when he got out of line. She also worked hard as a laundress, sometimes picking up wash from her employers and other times going to their houses. On the latter occasions, she took Louis and Beatrice with her rather than leave them unattended.

New Orleans at that time was notorious for its illicit nightlife, especially in a downtown area commonly referred to as "the District" (short for "red-light district") and later known as Storyville. It was divided into two segregated sections. "White" Storyville was lined with luxurious restaurants and casinos operated by New Orleans's unique population of "Creoles of color"—people of mixed black and French or Spanish extraction. The main attraction was swanky brothels, such as Lulu White's Mahogany Hall, where elegant prostitutes entertained high-paying white customers.

South of Canal Street, Storyville became a different place, equally active but much less glamorous. "Black" Storyville also had prostitutes, but they lured customers into "cribs," cement barracks situated on unpaved streets alongside ramshackle bars and dance halls. Families lived there, too, typically in one-story structures about 25 feet square, with an outhouse in back and no indoor plumbing; residents got their water from outdoor cisterns that filled up with rainwater. To bathe, they boiled water, poured it into a tub, then crouched inside, scrubbing wherever they could reach.

The population of Black Storyville included many criminals who carried on so violently that the neighborhood was nicknamed the Battlefield. Jane Alley, the street where Louis was born, stood at the center of this activity. "In that one block between Gravier and Perdido Streets more people were crowded than you ever saw in your life," he maintained. "There were churchpeople, gamblers, hustlers, cheap pimps, thieves, prostitutes, and lots of children. There were bars, honky-tonks [dance halls] and saloons, and lots of women walking the streets for tricks to take to their 'pads,' as they called their rooms."

Louis attended school, but like most young children in Storyville, he preferred to be on the street, playing with friends or scrounging for money. After school and on weekends, he earned pennies by scavenging for bits of brass and for tinfoil discarded from cigarette packs. He peddled these goods to junk dealers.

A more strenuous task was pounding red bricks into powder, then lugging bucketfuls of the stuff to prostitutes. They stirred ocher or urine into the granules, forming a shiny mix that they rubbed onto the

Unlike their white counterparts, the black prostitutes in Black Storyville lived and worked in squalid conditions. They dwelled in "cribs" along unpaved streets, which turned to mud when it rained, and went without a sewer system until late in the 19th century.

stoops of their houses to make them look more inviting. For a bucketful of dust Louis received a nickel, the price of a movie ticket. When he was older, he contributed to the family's income by hawking newspapers and running errands for prostitutes and other adults who hung out on the street.

Louis grew up bounded by poverty. As a child, he went barefoot year-round, gathering cuts and blisters, his skinny limbs clad in oversized hand-me-downs borrowed from his mother's boyfriends. His meals were meager recyclings of rice, beans, gumbo (okra trimmed with seafood bits), and a gristly chowder called fish-head stew. His diet was so poor, in fact, that it improved dramatically when his mother briefly dated a restaurant employee who brought home leftovers scraped off the plates of sated diners.

Decades later, Louis recalled his childhood so fondly that we might never guess how difficult life in the early 1900s was for him and for any ghetto black in the Deep South. In fact, these were among the leanest times in the history of black America. Second-class citizenship was forced on blacks by Jim Crow laws, which functioned much like South Africa's apartheid, limiting blacks to inferior neighborhoods and schools. And unwritten codes kept blacks in low-paying and backbreaking jobs, under the thumb of cruel and even sadistic white bosses. Acts of violent racism occurred almost daily.

Louis had his share of frightening episodes. One happened in the summer of 1912, when he and some friends decided to take a swim in a local pond. The group was "having a lot of fun," according to Louis, "when [his friend] Jimmy's bathing trunks fell off. While we were hurrying to fish them out of the water a white man took a shot gun off the rack on [his] porch. As Jimmy was struggling frantically to pull his trunks on again the white man aimed the shot gun at him." The man eventually put down his gun and laughed, as if the boys' terror were a grand joke. "We were scared stiff," Louis later admitted.

Racism was so rampant that blacks drew whatever solace they could from humor and wit, and from music, which in New Orleans enjoyed a long and hallowed tradition. Not long after French colonists founded the city in the mid-18th century, it gained a reputation as the citadel of American music. By the 19th century, New Orleans boasted the country's best opera company and its largest supply of professional orchestras and amateur marching bands.

The local police force outfitted a band and so did the fire department. And music rinsed the dusty thoroughfares and byways of the ghetto. On street corners, in cafés, and in steamy honky-tonks, the strains of marching tunes, dance melodies, blues, and the new Kansas City import, ragtime, punctuated the days and reverberated late into the night, distilling the rhythms of Storyville's daily dramas.

Even funerals inspired hot playing. When a local resident died, a uniformed band trudged behind the coffin, intoning mournful hymns all the way to the

During Armstrong's youth in New Orleans, the air was filled with music from a variety of activities, including funeral struts like this one. The men dressed in street clothes belong to the procession's "second line" and are hangers-on, trailing the band from the cemetery to Storyville.

black cemetery, located several miles from Storyville. Once the corpse was laid to rest, the band left its sorrow at the grave and sauntered smartly back to town playing lively songs. By the time the procession, or "strut," reached Storyville, the players were going at full throttle, and a crowd of hangers-on trailed in their wake. People packed the streets to applaud.

The competition for audiences was so fierce that rival bands often staged contests. If two groups happened to be booked in different clubs on a given night, each set of players would clamber into its own horse-drawn wagon and head off for an impromptu duel, or battle, held on a neutral street corner. Listeners gathered, and their applause determined the winner. If both bands excelled, bystanders locked the two wagons together by chaining their wheels, forcing the musicians to play on.

This competitive atmosphere drove the musicians to remarkable displays of skill and to upgrade their traditional fare until it took on a sparkling new shape. Day by day, New Orleans street musicians were developing a unique type of music, Dixieland, that ingeniously blended many familiar forms: ragtime, blues, hymns, and marching tunes—even European orchestral and chamber pieces learned by a few Creole artists who performed at private parties hosted by wealthy whites. No one consciously decided to unite these many different strands. Musicians simply used every available source to improve what they were already playing.

Day and night, Louis drank in these sounds. Their brassy blare offered a diversion from the hardship of the ghetto and also offered a wordless code to the alluring secrets of the adult world. Peering into the darkened windows of honky-tonks, he spied a microcosm of that world—dockworkers, hoodlums, prostitutes, and more—all swaying to the fiery playing of Buddy Bolden, Bunk Johnson, Joseph "King" Oliver,

and other masters of the cornet (a stubby version of the trumpet). Like many young boys, Louis envisioned himself triumphing at a duel between soloists (known as a cutting contest), thrilling the patrons of a dance hall, and parading in a smart band uniform through Storyville's crowded streets.

Hungry to make music but far too poor to buy a cornet, Louis began to perform on the instrument he was born with—his voice—and at the age of 10, he joined a quartet that vocalized for pennies on street corners. The group stuck together for two or three years, singing several times a week. This constituted Louis's first musical training. He had to learn many tunes, and for each a specific vocal part. This required patience, a keen ear, and the ability to harmonize. The money he earned helped support his mother and sister.

Performing also kept Louis on the street, where trouble lurked in many guises: He was surrounded by

While growing up, Armstrong was often immersed in the sounds of Dixieland. A traditional form of jazz, Dixieland evolved from many different kinds of music— especially the sharply accented rhythms of ragtime, which was performed by bands such as this one in early 20th-century New Orleans.

One of the top cornetists in New Orleans, Joe "King" Oliver helped mold Dixieland into a sophisticated art form. He also played a major role in Armstrong's development as a musician.

a world of vice and crime. The quartet usually sang at night, when Storyville buzzed with locals and visitors in the mood for entertainment. Competition among street acts was intense, so Louis and his group perfected strategies for attracting listeners.

One plan was for the lead singer and the tenor—Louis himself—to amble along the street ahead of the bass and the baritone. All of them sang, but seemingly to amuse only themselves, as if unaware that anyone might overhear them. Eventually, someone hailed one of the group and urged him to perform. Immediately, all the boys convened, and a small crowd gathered as the quartet ran through some of its specialties. Afterward, they passed around a hat, and because the boys were talented, appreciative listeners tossed in coins. "Most of the time we would draw down a nice little taste," Louis said. "Then I would make a bee line for home and dump my share into mama's lap."

Louis did not always use his time so productively. The teeming streets held temptations for a poor boy. He occasionally hustled money from adults, most likely gullible strangers who came to Storyville to sample its illicit pleasures. And now and again he stole: a piece of fruit from an inattentive vendor, an article of clothing from a bin. Even the booty that never made it into the family till eased the financial burden borne by his mother.

To discerning eyes, Louis seemed headed for a bad end. He was footloose most hours of the day and night, received little supervision at home, and began to flirt with criminality—or so the New Orleans Police Department concluded after an incident that occurred on New Year's Eve in 1912 or 1913.

In Storyville, people greeted the new year with noisy exuberance, discharging fireworks and firearms. Louis's quartet planned to sing that night, and he brought along a .38-caliber pistol, loaded with blanks, that he had discovered in a trunk belonging to his mother's latest boyfriend. As the group crossed Rampart Street, singing a hit tune, a youngster on the opposite corner fired a gun in their direction—either a cap gun or a real one; accounts differ.

Urged by his friends to retaliate, Louis drew his gun and pulled the trigger. The .38's booming report terrified Louis's antagonist and delighted his friends, who wanted to hear more. Louis prepared to oblige them when, as he said later, "all of a sudden two white arms hugged me, and I looked up and there was a big tall policeman. Boy, I thought the world was coming to an end."

In fact, it was just beginning. ❦

3

HARD LESSONS

———— ❦ ————

LOUIS'S PLEAS THAT he had meant no harm fell on deaf—and, perhaps, deafened—ears. He was hauled to the New Orleans Juvenile Court and brought before a judge. Under different circumstances, the young offender might have received a stern lecture, then been released to the custody of his parents, who would have been trusted to mete out the appropriate punishment. But this was the Deep South in the early 1900s, and Louis was completely at the mercy of the court. It sentenced him to an indefinite stay in a detention center.

Louis spent the night in a jail cell and the next morning was herded into a police wagon along with several other boys. A heavy door slammed shut, and a rhythmic clopping of hooves sounded as the horse-drawn wagon lurched off. They passed through New Orleans's busy streets, then through quieter outlying neighborhoods, and finally left the city altogether at some point—exactly where, it was impossible to guess because the only view the boys had was between the iron bars of a tiny window.

At last the wagon halted, and Louis and the others climbed out. They were miles from the city, on a country road. On one side stretched acres of dairy land where horses and cattle calmly grazed. Across

---

Armstrong (circled) joined his first instrumental group, the Colored Waifs' Home Band, when he was 14 years old. Shortly after taking up the cornet, he was appointed the band's leader.

COLORED   WAIFS' (Jones')   HOME
   1913   New Orleans, Louisiana   1913

The greenery on the grounds of the Colored Waifs' Home offered Armstrong a pleasing contrast to the fetid and teeming streets of his native Black Storyville. Joseph Jones (inset), who headed the home, was one of the most innovative social workers in New Orleans.

the way, tall trees stood guard before a dilapidated building, two stories high, that housed a dormitory, classroom, chapel, and mess hall. This was the Colored Waifs' Home, run by Joseph and Manuella Jones, black social workers who had won a citywide reputation for reforming wayward children. Louis entered the grounds and caught his first glimpse of honeysuckle shrubs, in bloom even though it was winter. Their flowers, shaped like the bells of tiny white trumpets, smelled sweetly of nectar.

Inside the home, Louis was led down a corridor and into the mess hall. A long line of inmates filed by a counter, where plain white rice was doled onto their plates. Louis had not eaten all day, but he was so unhappy that his usually robust appetite deserted him and he pushed his meal away. He refused to eat during the next three days as well, but on the fourth morning he was famished and beat everyone else to the table.)

Joseph Jones, a retired army captain, staunchly believed in military discipline. He ran the home like a boot camp. Each dawn, the boys awoke to the strains of a bugle, and they were similarly summoned to meals and to their bunks at the end of the exhausting day. Strict rules regulated work, study, and play. Troublemakers, especially runaways, were punished promptly. Once they were caught, they were ordered to strip off all of their clothing, then were whipped so badly that they could not sit for weeks. The boys even drilled in formation, shouldering wooden guns.

More practical instruction included lessons in the three R's, taught by the all-black staff, and in gardening and carpentry. And there were many chores. The boys chopped firewood and lit flames under the huge kettle in which they boiled their dirty clothes.

As rigorous as the routine was, it left room for enjoyment. The quiet countryside—its generous open spaces, grazing animals, massed greenery—differed agreeably from the crowded frenzy of Storyville, with its sudden bursts of violence, its foul backyard privies, its jostling and hustling. And though the staff at the home was strict, they were fair-minded for the most part. To Louis, their evident concern came as a welcome change from Willie Armstrong's vanishing act and from the bored or cruel behavior of the men who drifted in and out of Mayann Armstrong's house.

Louis missed his friends, especially his pals in the quartet, but he found companionship in the home. The easygoing manner that had charmed the inhabitants of Storyville and earned him the nickname "Dippermouth" made him equally popular in the Colored Waifs' Home. The other boys quickly discovered that Louis would never tattle and that he suffered with the rest when a runaway was caught and dealt his painful punishment.

Louis's diligence, alertness, and enthusiasm also won the affection of the staff, with one exception: Peter Davis. He distrusted boys from tough neighborhoods, and the Battlefield was the toughest in New Orleans. From the start, Louis feared that Davis had it in for him. And after the teacher dealt him 15 hard lashes for a minor infraction early in his stay, Louis tried to keep his distance.

But it was not easy to do—not only because the staff kept a close watch on the boys but also because in addition to teaching vocational training, Davis directed the Colored Waifs' Home Band. This was a musical group composed entirely of inmates who received daily lessons, practiced regularly, and—best of all—performed all over New Orleans, in white neighborhoods and black. As soon as Louis learned about the band, he ached to join it. But he was too scared to approach Davis. Whenever Louis loitered near the rehearsals, staring longingly at the musicians and imbibing the sounds they made, the director either ignored him altogether or scowled forbiddingly.

Still, Louis could not keep away. All the Dixieland he had heard in Storyville and his success with the quartet had whetted his appetite to play. He even wished he could trade places with the boy who tumbled out of his cot at daybreak to wake the others with his bugle calls. By this time, Louis knew what instrument he wanted to learn: the cornet, whose tones had been embedded in his memory by Bunk Johnson, Joe Oliver, and other Storyville stars who led funeral struts and dueled in spectacular cutting contests.

Gradually, as Louis proved he was not just another hoodlum from Perdido Street, Davis began to relent, and now and then favored Louis with an encouraging smile. And one day, after Louis had sung with a group organized by another teacher, Davis asked him if he would like to join the brass band. Louis was speechless.

Davis repeated the question, and Louis managed to stammer, "Yes."

At last—six months after arriving at the home—Louis would hold a cornet in his hands, finger the valves, blow his first notes, shape his first melody. "I thought of what the gang would say when they saw me pass through the neighborhood blowing a cornet," he said later. "I already pictured myself playing with all the power and endurance of a Bunk [Johnson], Joe [Oliver], or [Buddy] Bolden." Flushed with excitement, he appeared at his first rehearsal, joining the boys he had envied for months. Davis then ceremoniously presented Louis with his first instrument: a tambourine.

Louis was deflated, but he betrayed no disappointment. Instead, he hefted the hand-sized instrument. When the band started up, he slapped his fingers against the taut circle of skin and shook the metal bangles looped to the wooden frame. He instantly matched the rhythm that the others were playing.

Impressed by this display, Davis switched Louis onto the drums as the band plunged into another song, a popular number called "At the Animals' Ball." Louis had memorized the band's entire repertory from his hours of secret listening, and he knew there was a drum solo. When his turn came, he pounded ferociously. The other boys cheered.

By now, Peter Davis was intrigued. He thrust yet another instrument into his new pupil's hands—this time an alto horn, a brass instrument often featured in marching bands. Though a horn player himself, Davis did not bother to instruct Louis in the complex mechanics of fingering, of positioning one's lips and tongue, of regulating one's breathing. Instead, he left this beginner entirely to his own devices. It was a kind of experiment, like putting a baseball bat in the hands of someone who has never played the game but who is a natural athlete. He is sure to crowd the plate, grip the bat awkwardly, and lunge at pitches

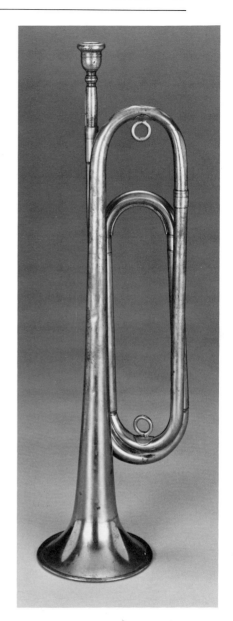

Armstrong played this bugle during his stay at the Colored Waifs' Home.

far outside the strike zone. But he is equally sure to make rapid, almost unconscious adjustments that no ordinary novice could ever make.

So it was with Louis. He had never held an alto horn, let alone tried to play one. It was larger than a cornet and differently shaped, but like a cornet it was mounted with three raised valves, each about a knuckle high, and it had a metal mouthpiece. Louis pressed his lips to it and blew, depressing the valves in an approximation of the fingerings he had seen practiced horn players make. The tones that came out fell within the range of his own voice, so he guessed the instrument took a part similar to that taken by the tenor in a vocal group.

When the band started up, Louis did his best to duplicate that remembered role. He probably managed few clean notes. But Peter Davis did not care. It was evident to him that for all Louis lacked in the way of expertise, he splendidly possessed something that could never be taught: talent. He had a marvelous ear for melody, harmony, and rhythm and a natural instinct for the blending of parts that made a band sound good. The undersized urchin from Storyville was a born musician.

Once his promise was recognized, Louis flourished. He progressed so quickly on the alto horn that within months he inherited the bugler's post when the boy who had held it was released from the home. Louis cherished the ancient instrument, polishing its tarnished brass until it shone. And the tones he coaxed from it were so lovely that Davis promoted him to its orchestral equivalent, the cornet, and then appointed him bandleader. Louis would now march at the head of the band.

For the first time in almost a year, Louis left the home and its pastoral grounds to lead the band in its parades through the city. Performances could be exhausting. Some days, the band covered 25 miles on foot without resting. And because they represented

the entire home, the band members were expected to be models of well-trained obedience, as if they were shouldering Joseph Jones's wooden rifles instead of musical instruments. Still, the chance to play the cornet and to spend long hours in New Orleans amply compensated for the exhaustion Louis felt at the end of each day.

A high point for Louis came when he returned to Storyville. His mother and his friends joined the crowd lining the streets as he marched by at the head of the troupe, wearing a uniform topped with the leader's cream-colored cap. Usually, the boys received peppermint candy and gingerbread cakes as a reward for playing. But the appearance of Louis in his old neighborhood caused such a sensation that the on-lookers took up a collection on the spot, filling several hats. The money went toward buying new instruments and outfits for the band.

As a member of the Colored Waifs' Home Band, Armstrong performed throughout the city of New Orleans. Shown here is Canal Street, which served as the dividing line between White and Black Storyville.

Day by day, Louis improved on the cornet. But even after he became the star of the Colored Waifs' Home Band, he had a long way to go as a musician. His natural gifts—as great as they were—emerged only crudely between the croaks, the fluffs, the missed beats. Each frustrating day of practice reminded him that he had chosen to master a tough instrument.

Because the cornet has only 3 valves to press down and then release, it may seem simple to play when compared, for instance, to a piano with its 88 keys. But the cornet poses a different kind of challenge to beginners, who must use their lips, tongue, and teeth to regulate the flow of air that passes through the instrument. They do this by building an *embouchure*, a positioning of the mouth against the sharp metal mouthpiece that can be rapidly adjusted to change the pitch and tone of individual notes. These adjustments must become second nature, like those that enable us to form different sounds when we speak.

The task is doubly trying without proper guidance. Most young New Orleans players had to struggle alone through their apprenticeship. But Louis was lucky; he came under the daily tutelage of Peter Davis. Although Davis was not a professional teacher schooled in the most advanced methods of instruction, he was an experienced horn player capable of demonstrating the rudiments of correct playing.

After months of study, Louis learned to create a full resonant tone, attacking each note firmly and accurately. He also discovered that, more than anything else, he wanted to become a professional musician.

After about two years in the home, Louis won his release through the efforts of an unexpected source: his father, who persuaded the juvenile court judge that if Louis were released, he would be returning to a secure household. This was not quite the fib it might seem. Neglectful as Willie Armstrong had been, he was at least dependably employed.

Louis left the home with mixed feelings. He was about 15 and eager to strike out on his own. Perhaps he could find a full-time job and help support his mother and sister. He would be back in Storyville again, amid the honky-tonks and the cafés and his old friends. He would be free. On the other hand, he had grown used to the home, to its routine, to the other "waifs" who had become his friends, and, above all, to the brass band. He would be leaving behind his cornet, his uniform, and his lessons with Peter Davis.

It was thus a bittersweet day in June 1914 when Willie Armstrong arrived to remove Louis from the home. He bade good-bye to Captain Jones and Peter Davis, shook hands with his fellow bandsmen, and for the last time inhaled the odor of the honeysuckle shrubs he had first breathed two years before. ✿

While Peter Davis (far right) was serving as Armstrong's first mentor, he noticed the young musician's penchant for showmanship. "At the first note of music," said the director of the Colored Waifs' Home Band, "he'd break into comedy dances. He could sing real well as a boy, too, even though his voice was coarse."

4

PLAYING FOR
KEEPS

◆

Ι̲T SEEMED STRANGE to Louis that his father had suddenly reentered his life. Unlike Mayann, who had paid regular visits to the Colored Waifs' Home, Willie Armstrong had not put in a single appearance there, which was hardly a surprise; he had ignored Louis since birth. Louis knew his father had started a second family in Black Storyville with a woman named Gertrude, who bore him two sons: Willie, Jr., and Henry. The busy household did not seem to lack for a new member.

But another member was exactly what the family needed. Both parents worked, and the two youngsters had no one to care for them during the day. That was where Louis came in. What better candidate for a live-in baby-sitter and housekeeper than half-brother Louis, who for two years had arisen at dawn to make his bed and boil his laundry? He became a cost-free household servant, charged with overseeing his half brothers.

Most teenagers would have despaired, but Louis bore his plight calmly. After all, he had more freedom than in the detention home, and his place in this new family was not entirely defined by the domestic chores he performed. His stepmother proved to be a warm and loving woman. Even his father recognized Louis's value and made an effort to treat him decently.

Best of all, yet another addition to the family— an infant born about a year after Louis arrived—left the Armstrongs with one too many mouths to feed. For all his usefulness, Louis did not bring in an in-

Armstrong at about the age of 20, in a formal portrait with his sister, Beatrice, and their mother.

Anxious to be hired as a musician in the late 1910s, Armstrong began to frequent the dance halls and saloons on Basin Street, in the heart of New Orleans's red-light district. He made these job-hunting excursions at night, after spending the entire day shoveling coal.

come. Consequently, Mayann appeared at the house one evening and, after a long consultation with Willie Armstrong, departed with her son. Louis barely hid his elation.

Back on Liberty and Perdido streets—his "old stomping grounds"—Louis looked up his old friends, who now wore long pants instead of knickers and held regular jobs in the neighborhood. The adult world he had spied through the knotholes of honky-tonks now beckoned to him, and he landed a job working for one of Mayann Armstrong's boyfriends. From 7:00 A.M. to 5:00 P.M., he shoveled coal into a large, mule-drawn wagon, then traveled through the city selling his cargo—about a ton of coal—for 15 cents a load. It was hard labor, and Louis, who was small for his age and skinny, never managed to fill and deliver more than 5 loads a day—a total day's earnings of 75 cents. This was not enough to support himself, Mayann, and his sister, who had grown big enough to have acquired the nickname "Mama Lucy."

Louis wanted to supplement his earnings, and the means for doing so seemed evident: He must play music professionally. Yet this was a daunting prospect. It was one thing to star with the Colored Waifs' Home Band, winning the applause of adults more attentive to the sight of uniformed delinquents marching in obedient ranks than to the sounds that issued from their battered instruments. It was quite another to take the stage before a paying audience. Louis did not even own a cornet.

On the other hand, Storyville's population of working musicians included many part-timers who possessed only rudimentary skills. The owners of honky-tonks, in particular, cared little about the quality of music provided by the bands they hired. Practically any player would do—as long as he put in long hours and accepted low wages.

Louis could easily join this company of marginal professionals. He had only, in the words of a savvy friend, to "put on [his] long pants and play the blues for the whores that hustle all night." Prostitutes preferred blues because their slow tempos suited the seductive dances—called "drags"—that they performed in the tight embrace of clients. Blues equally suited the skills of a beginning cornetist. They had regular tempos, repetitive melodies, and required no more of a soloist than that he memorize a limited number of stock phrases.

Several nights a week—after long hours of hauling coal—Louis made the rounds, looking to sit in with some of the local bands. Usually, he found at least one combo whose cornetist, ready for a breather, gladly vacated his chair for the session. Before long, Louis became a familiar face in Storyville's honky-tonks.

For an all-night session, Louis usually pocketed about a dollar plus tips, forked over by generous customers who liked his cheerful, energetic manner and his wide toothy smile. Money in hand, he trudged home for a few hours' sleep, then headed off at dawn with his coal wagon. It was a grueling routine, but he was, in his own words, "young, strong and had all the ambition in the world and I wanted to do a lot to help Mayann and Mama Lucy."

He was also obsessed. The more Louis played, the more he enjoyed it, and the more he became driven to excel. He had no chance of doing so if he continued to rely on rented instruments. They sufficed for gigs but then had to be returned, leaving him with nothing to practice on. So he scraped together $10 and splurged on his first cornet, a homely relic that had been gathering dust in a pawnshop.

Hungry for pointers, Louis attached himself to the city's more experienced players, although most New Orleans veterans jealously guarded their wisdom. The stingiest of all was cornetist Freddie Keppard, who covered the valves of his instrument with a handkerchief so rival musicians could not see what

New Orleans–based trumpeter Freddie Keppard (right) was one of the greatest performers in the early days of jazz. He was also among the most jealous: He hid the secrets of his unique playing style from other musicians.

Kid Ory's Sunshine Orchestra, shown here in 1919, featured the cornet playing of Mutt Carey (second from left), the New Orleans blues star who became one of Armstrong's earliest fans.

notes he played. This was an act of vanity rather than a realistic precaution. A talented player—especially Louis, who had a faultless ear—did not need to see the valves as they were pressed. Once he heard a series of notes, he committed them to memory and later worked out the fingering for himself.

Louis's rapid progress as a blues player received unexpected confirmation one day in New Orleans's Lincoln Park. The young cornetist went there to hear Edward "Kid" Ory, a trombonist who led one of the top bands in the city. Ory had two brilliant cornetists. One of them was Mutt Carey, who took a break during the performance and yielded his chair to Armstrong. Years later, Carey said of the incident, "Every time he played a chorus it was different and [yet] you knew it was the blues. . . . When he got through playing . . . I kidded him a little. I told him, 'Louis, you keep playing that horn and some day you'll be a great man.' "

Carey was not alone in perceiving the promise in this beginner. The other cornetist in Ory's band was equally impressed. His name was Joe Oliver.

The facts of Joe Oliver's origins are murky, but he seems to have been born on a farm outside New Orleans in about 1880. As a child, he was sent to the city and placed in the care of a well-to-do Jewish family who raised him and also trained him as a household servant. Once he came of age, he worked full-time as a butler and gardener for various white families in New Orleans.

Oliver gravitated toward music in his youth, taking up first the trombone, which he quickly abandoned, then the cornet, which he stuck with and slowly mastered. (He later admitted that he struggled with the instrument for 10 years before developing a good tone.) During this time, he landed part-time gigs with local combos and held down a day job as a domestic servant.

Oliver's first break came in 1912, when Kid Ory needed a replacement for his star cornetist, Freddie Keppard, a heavy drinker who had become unmanageable. Ory, who had the pick of New Orleans horn players, chose Oliver. The partnership began stormily; both Ory and Oliver had domineering personalities and clashed frequently. In Ory's words, Oliver "was as rough as pig-iron."

Soon after his talent was tapped by Ory, Oliver began to branch out, organizing bands of his own that won a following throughout the city. Dixieland was then taking shape as a musical form, and Oliver had definite ideas about how it ought to be played. He favored a highly disciplined sound with clean melodic lines traded by the cornet and clarinet. He also was an exacting, inflexible, occasionally abusive leader, not above cheating the other players out of their earnings and bullying them with his imposing height and chesty bulk.

Oliver's forceful leadership contrasted vividly with the sounds that issued from his cornet. They were gentle and sweet, softened by the balled-up rag that he pressed into the bell of the instrument.

Restraint also governed Oliver's offstage life. As soon as a show ended, he packed up his instrument and returned to the sedate life he shared with his wife and stepdaughter. He disdained the carousing enjoyed by many musicians, and he seldom drank. His only indulgence was food. He consumed it in legendary quantities—six hamburgers at a sitting, according to one account.

By about 1916, Oliver stood at the pinnacle of New Orleans's cornetists and bandleaders. He was in demand all over the city, including the choice clubs of White Storyville. Other musicians were eager to learn from him, especially Louis Armstrong, who decided to place himself directly under the wing of the older man. Luckily for the young cornetist, the world of Storyville was small and informal, so opportunities often arose for him to study his hero.

Oliver regularly performed at Pete Lala's, a popular cabaret where he had a standing engagement. Too young to enter the establishment, Armstrong nonetheless contrived a unique way to begin his apprenticeship. One of his coal customers, a prostitute, lived next door to Lala's, and he grabbed every chance to drive his delivery wagon to her place. "I'd just stand in that lady's crib listening to King Oliver," he said. "All of a sudden it would dawn on the lady that I was still in her crib very silent . . . and she'd say— 'What's the matter with you boy? . . . Why are you still standing so quiet?' And there I'd have to explain to her that I was being inspired by *the* [Joe] Oliver and his orchestra."

Just as Armstrong eventually earned the favor of Peter Davis, so he charmed Oliver, becoming part disciple, part mascot. Armstrong later said that when Oliver "went into a bar to yackety with the guys— he didn't drink—or when he'd be parading and not blowing, I'd hold his horn so all he had to do was wipe his brow and walk."

Oliver, at first amused and flattered by Armstrong, soon became intrigued. After his sessions at Lala's, he ambled by Henry Matranga's honky-tonk, where Armstrong sat in with a band. All the players were good, but Oliver recognized that the young cornetist bristled with talent. Oliver broke with New Orleans tradition—and with his own standoffish

Armstrong, at age 22, strikes an unusually tough pose with Joe Oliver in Chicago. In actuality, it was Oliver—not Armstrong— who bullied his colleagues. Although an extremely talented cornetist, he was a hot-tempered, domineering bandleader.

manner—by inviting Armstrong to his house. There the two feasted on red beans and rice—Armstrong's favorite repast—then practiced cornet duets, using an exercise book. Thus, Armstrong learned some fine points about fingering and tone.

In 1917, the fortunes of New Orleans, the course of jazz, and the direction of Armstrong's life all took an unexpected turn. On April 6, the United States entered World War I, joining the alliance headed by England and France, which had been battling against the German empire since 1914. War preparations began with a massive military draft that drew nearly 3 million Americans into the army. Others voluntarily enlisted in the national guard, the marine corps, and the navy. This last armed service sent several thousand young men to New Orleans, which, as one of America's largest ports, had facilities adequate for the housing and training of apprentice sailors.

Like servicemen everywhere, those posted in New Orleans explored the local nightlife, and the delta city offered many temptations: hot music, good food, and, especially, a large population of prostitutes. Every night, a navy-blue horde, released from the rigors of military training, stormed the showplaces north of Canal Street and the cement barracks of Black Storyville. Alarm spread through the U.S. Navy Department, whose officials feared for the health and morals of the country's troops and pressed for the district to be closed. Local leaders protested that outlawing the trade would simply drive it underground and make it more difficult to control. But the navy brass prevailed, and on November 12, 1917, Storyville effectively went out of business—not only the sanctioned places of prostitution but the related establishments it supported: hotels, restaurants, cabarets, and dance halls.

Dixieland musicians, watching their incomes dwindle, realized the time had come for them to test the new music outside New Orleans. The final im-

petus to leave the city came when a group of white New Orleans musicians called the Original Dixieland Jass Band (ODJB) landed a gig in Reisenweber's, a New York City restaurant, in 1917. Diners loved the new sound—or, at least, ODJB's watered-down version of it. The Victor recording company signed the band to a contract, and its first disk—"Livery Stable Blues" backed by "Original Dixieland One-Step"— sold in the millions. America, it seemed, was poised to embrace the New Orleans sound.

The Original Dixieland Jass Band was hardly original, despite its claim that it invented jazz. In fact, it simply imitated the sounds of other Dixieland bands, such as Kid Ory's and Joe Oliver's. Yet it was the first jazz group to make a recording, which whetted the nation's appetite for more jazz.

5

BEYOND
NEW ORLEANS

IN 1917, BIG-NAME players departed from New Orleans in droves. One of the few holdouts was Joe Oliver, until he soured on the raunchy New Orleans scene and accepted a spot with a band in Chicago. A crowd gathered at the train station to see the great man off. Armstrong was there, of course. He later described the farewell as "a rather sad parting. [Oliver] really didn't want to leave New Orleans, and I felt the old gang was breaking up."

Armstrong's spirits lifted, however, when he learned he had been chosen by Kid Ory to replace Oliver. "What a thrill that was!" Armstrong said. "To think I was considered up to taking Joe Oliver's place in the best band in town! I couldn't hardly wait to get to Mayann's place to tell her the good news."

Small talents shine when surrounded by mediocrity; large talents prosper from competition. As a member of the Kid Ory Band, Armstrong would be tested almost nightly by top players, the best who remained in New Orleans after the northern exodus began. Shy as he was, awed as he was by the prospect of replacing Oliver, Armstrong felt equal to the demands of Ory's band. But before he won New Orleans jazz fans over, he had to persuade his new colleagues that he belonged in the band.

Armstrong left the New Orleans vicinity for the first time in 1918, when he joined Fate Marable's orchestra, which played on riverboats that paddled up the Mississippi River. Along with Armstrong, other notable members of the band were Johnny St. Cyr on banjo and Baby Dodds on drums.

Armstrong's first gig with the Kid Ory Band was at a big place called Economy Hall. He mounted the stand wearing a towel around his neck, as Oliver did. And when the band swung into their repertoire, Armstrong not only kept up with them easily, he also duplicated Oliver's beautiful solos. As he later said, "I'd listened to Joe all the time he was with Kid Ory [and] I knew everything that band played. . . . I was pretty fast on my horn at that time, and I had a good ear. I could catch on real fast."

Armstrong supplemented his work with the Kid Ory Band by playing in the few honky-tonks that, in defiance of the 1917 law, still operated in New Orleans and its environs. Disreputable places in the days of legalized prostitution, the tonks became even tougher after the law changed. An especially dangerous tonk was the Brick House, in the nearby town of Gretna. On Saturday nights, it was packed with hard-drinking dockworkers who carried knives and guns and often crowned one another with empty bottles. Prostitutes prowled the dance floor, swaying to the thumping rhythm of the blues. Armstrong played there often in 1918.

One of the women who regularly worked the floor at the Brick House was Daisy Parker, a petite and comely 21-year-old whose eyes wandered in Armstrong's direction. He returned her glances, and one dawn, after his show ended, he joined her in one of the tonk's upstairs rooms. They met again the next weekend and the next, slipping upstairs for trysts that lasted until late in the afternoon.

The couple continued in this way for weeks. Then the Kid Ory Band landed a lucrative Saturday-night gig playing for white audiences at the New Orleans Country Club. A month passed during which Armstrong's only contact with Daisy Parker came via the telephone. Desperate to see her again, he rode a bus out to Freetown, the rural hamlet where Daisy lived, only to discover that she shared the place with another man who did not take kindly to Armstrong's intrusion. For his part, Armstrong resented being Daisy's side dish. He scurried back to New Orleans, deciding, as he put it, "to give her up as a bad job."

A month or more passed. Armstrong stewed about the rude jolt Daisy had given him, and she seemed to have erased him from her life. Then, one day she suddenly appeared on Perdido Street. He greeted her warily, but she sailed into his arms, and his defenses wilted.

Reunited, the pair became not only lovers but intimate friends, although they were a match of opposites. Armstrong was good-natured, disciplined, industrious, and cheerful in the face of extreme hardship. Daisy was selfish, sharp-tongued, and spoiled, having been raised by doting parents who indulged her shamelessly. They let her play hooky from school, so she never learned to read and write, and she showed no interest in acquiring these skills. Worse, she was hot tempered and frequently flew into violent rages. But, as Armstrong said much later, "It's a funny thing about two people being in love—whatever little traits there are, no matter how unpleasant they may be, love will drown them out."

The pair married in 1918. They nested in two rooms above an upholstery establishment. To reach the apartment, they climbed a stairway that rose up steeply from a filthy alley. Like many flats in Storyville tenements, the Armstrongs' place opened onto porches (called "galleries" in New Orleans). One porch was in such disrepair that it sagged and thus acted as a duct for rainwater, which seeped into the Armstrongs' quarters and mingled with the rank odor of the backyard garbage carelessly tossed by tenants and the landlord. It was not a romantic home, but like most newlyweds, the Armstrongs were glad simply to have a place of their own.

This house is nearly identical to the place where Armstrong lived with his wife Daisy in New Orleans. A staircase climbs steeply to a second-floor flat, and an open-air "gallery" peers over a trash-filled alley.

Armstrong (second from left) with his cousin Clarence Miles (far right), who became the musician's lifelong ward. They are shown here with the leader of the Zulus, a prominent social club for New Orleans blacks, and his son.

Marital life proved trying, however. It took little to light Daisy's fuse, especially when she suspected her husband of infidelity. One time, when she saw him on the street with another woman, she pulled out a razor and charged at him. Armstrong leaped over a ditch and cleared it but lost his hat, an expensive Stetson bought with many months' savings. Daisy snatched it up and sliced it to shreds while her husband looked on in dismay.

There were more serious incidents. One occurred shortly after the couple moved into their flat. Because Armstrong was steadily employed, he was in a position to assist his relatives, and he agreed to care for his three-year-old cousin Clarence. The tot, who had an insatiable appetite for mischief, soon tired of the toys that the Armstrongs bought for him and busied himself by exploring his new home.

One rainy day, Clarence quietly played in the kitchen, to the relief of the married couple, who relaxed in their front room to the sounds of their Victrola. Suddenly, sharp cries penetrated the music and the clatter of falling rain. The Armstrongs dashed into the kitchen but could not find Clarence. Nor was he on the porch.

In a panic, Armstrong peered through the mist to the ground below. Clarence had slipped off the wet porch and had plunged headfirst to the hard ground. He now wobbled up the steps, clasping his head, a dazed expression on his face. He had sustained permanent brain damage.

Chaos ruled Armstrong's home life, but order governed his music. Pushed to new limits by the Kid Ory Band, he acquired greater resources for channeling the tumult of his life into eloquent musical expression. The inspired youth ripened into a mature artist.

In 1918, Armstrong came to the attention of Fate Marable, a bandleader whose group played atop the *Sidney*, one of several riverboats that in warm weather

Armstrong's first full-time gig was on the Sidney, *a riverboat that steamed up the mighty Mississippi on day excursions. The steady work, which lasted through the summer of 1921, greatly enhanced his cornet playing.*

left New Orleans for day cruises along the Mississippi River. Propelled by enormous paddle wheels, the boats served as floating entertainment palaces. Some even made summer-long excursions, paddling as far north as Duluth, Minnesota—more than 1,000 miles away. On these lengthy excursions, the boat dropped anchor each day at another town or city, picking up a load of travelers who danced and dined until nightfall, when the shore lights flickered on the dark river. At day's end, the boat returned to port and pressed on to the next town upriver.

Armstrong leaped at the chance to join Marable's band. It was full-time work—the best available to New Orleans players. It would also temporarily free him from the coal cart.

The riverboats added the final touches to Armstrong's playing. Customers expected sedate dance music rather than the standard Dixieland repertoire, and the band had to master many unfamiliar tunes. This meant studying sheet music, a skill Armstrong had not yet learned, although he was slightly ac-

quainted with musical notation from the instruction
Joe Oliver had given him from exercise books. A
fellow riverboat musician, David Jones, taught Armstrong how to read the sheet music that Marable
circulated among the players. Aided once again by
his marvelous ear, Armstrong caught on quickly. Soon,
he could deliver a new melody after a single run-
through.

However, Armstrong did not need any assistance
on his solos. By this time, he was improvising as well
as anyone in New Orleans, drawing on an assortment
of phrases borrowed from blues, Dixieland, and
marching tunes. On some songs, he added his own
inventions. Years later, when New Orleans musicians
recalled the birth and evolution of jazz, they often
pointed to the remarkable solos Armstrong devised
on the riverboats. It was said he could start a solo 10
miles outside a city and still be improvising when the
boat glided into the dock.

In 1920, Armstrong graduated from day excursions to summer-long trips that forced him to spend

months apart from his wife. He scarcely minded the separation. He had never been outside New Orleans and he enjoyed seeing new places. As the riverboat glided north, the vast continent unfolded: The marshy delta of Louisiana gave way to the fertile bluegrass of western Tennessee and Kentucky and then to the cosmopolitan grandeur of St. Louis. Next came Iowa and Illinois, midwestern states that had never known slavery and where only a generation before, German and Scandinavian immigrants had erected homesteads amid seas of rich farmland.

In 1922, Armstrong received his first invitation to leave his hometown permanently. The offer came from a New York City bandleader, Fletcher Henderson, whose touring group, the Black Swan Troubadours, stopped for a few nights in New Orleans. Henderson was avid for talent, and when he heard Armstrong play in a local club, he immediately tried to sign him up. Armstrong insisted that his best friend, drummer Zutty Singleton, be invited along as well. Henderson refused, and Armstrong stayed behind. The two would later unite under much different circumstances.

That same year, another offer came, this time by telegram. It was sent by Joe Oliver, who was leading the Creole Jazz Band in Chicago. He had decided to add a second cornet to his combo and summoned his protégé. "I always knew," Armstrong said later, "if I'm going to get a little break in this game, it was gonna be through Joe, nobody else."

Decades later, Armstrong admitted that Oliver's offer "scared [me] to death." Once again, it seemed he had been given the nod over more experienced players. Moreover, Oliver's band was generally thought to be the best in Chicago and, by extension, in the entire country.

Armstrong had silenced his own doubts before. This time, however, much more was at stake. He would be 900 miles from home—far from the familiar sights, sounds, and faces of his hometown. He could not find solace in Mayann's kitchen, nor reclaim his job on the coal cart. In Chicago, no one would know him as "Little Louis," Joe Oliver's likable sidekick, smiling with delight because the great man let him carry his horn. "I used to see so many kids leave New Orleans," Armstrong later remarked, "and they'd be gone for a long time, and then you look around they have to hobo their way back home." The same fate might befall him.

Nonetheless, Armstrong knew he could not spurn Oliver's invitation. The great man was Armstrong's hero, the musician whose approval meant the most to him. Only a coward would refuse to take this next step. Besides, New Orleans offered only limited opportunities, even to a cornetist who played with the best bands in the city. To remain there would mean a lifetime of winter day-jobs, of Saturday-night gigs in honky-tonks, of grueling funeral marches. The 23 year old from Storyville knew his moment had come.

Armstrong's wife had a different opinion. Daisy's life revolved around New Orleans and Storyville, and Chicago seemed impossibly distant. The couple quarreled and parted, and their stormy marriage collapsed. Armstrong returned to the home of the person who had always encouraged and comforted him—his mother. She urged him to accept Oliver's offer.

On August 8, 1922, Armstrong boarded a train in New Orleans, carrying two cases: One held a few changes of clothes—all he owned; the other held his cornet. He wore a coarse, stiff suit, a straw hat, and a layer of sweat—Mayann had made him don long underwear to avoid catching a chill on the northbound train. She had also packed for him a huge fish sandwich that had to last the entire journey because blacks were barred from the dining car, thanks to Jim Crow laws.

Armstrong first arrived in Chicago in 1922, just as jazz was becoming nationally popular. He quickly adapted to the playing style of Joe Oliver's Creole Jazz Band but had a more difficult time adjusting to the pace of life in the northern city, which was much faster than that of his hometown, New Orleans.

According to Armstrong, when he arrived at Illinois Central Station in Chicago, it was nearing midnight and no one was there to meet him. It was his own fault. He had missed the train Oliver had instructed him to take, and Oliver himself was busy at an engagement at his usual place: the Lincoln Gardens, a popular black dance hall on the south side of town.

Alone in the huge city, Armstrong panicked. He later said, "I saw a million people, but not Mister Joe, and I didn't give a damn who else was there. I said, no, this is the wrong city. I was just fixing to take the next train back home."

The young musician was rescued by a baggage handler who steered him toward a taxi that took him to the Lincoln Gardens. Whizzing through the Chicago streets, Armstrong was amazed by what he saw:

the furious traffic, the crowded sidewalks, and the towering skyscrapers, which he mistook for universities. The Lincoln Gardens was no less intimidating. Recently remodeled, it wore an elegant facade and a long canopy. The hall was spacious enough to hold 1,000 customers, who paid to watch a show that featured singers, entertainers, and bands, each introduced by a master of ceremonies. The prime attraction was Joe Oliver's Creole Jazz Band.

The band was in the middle of a number when Armstrong entered the vast hall. The contrast between the onstage players—his new colleagues—and himself was embarrassing. Oliver, recently nicknamed "the King," looked truly regal in his expensive suit and tie. The other musicians, all New Orleans natives whom Armstrong had met or played with, also exuded big-city confidence. There was Honore Dutrey, a trombonist; Baby Dodds, a drummer; banjoist Johnny St. Cyr; and clarinetist Johnny Dodds, who sported a diamond ring that flashed when his fingers reeled off dazzling runs.

Armstrong stood in the wings, listening. He had never heard music sound so good. Oliver's muted leads had grown tighter and sweeter, and the others matched him, handling their parts with tremendous skill. Armstrong feared that he could never keep up.

The set ended, and Armstrong edged toward the stage. The band crowded around to welcome him. All the band members were there except for pianist Lil Hardin, a slim young woman from Memphis, Tennessee, who had temporarily left the group.

Armstrong filled in his acquaintances on doings in New Orleans. Oliver then led him to a rented room in a boardinghouse run by a woman from New Orleans. Armstrong marveled at the luxury of this place; there was even a private bathtub. He soaked in it for hours, washing off the last traces of New Orleans. ❧

6

THE SOLOIST AND
THE SHOWMAN

IN THE EARLY 1920s, Chicago had about 3 million inhabitants, more than any city in America except New York. As an industrial center, Chicago had few rivals. Its railroad network, livestock and grain markets, and meat-packing companies led the world and employed a diverse array of ethnic groups: immigrants fresh off the boat from Italy, Czechoslovakia, and Poland; second- and third-generation German, Swedish, and Irish Americans; and more than 100,000 blacks, part of the huge migration that flooded out of the South in the early 1900s.

Southern blacks often called Chicago "the top of the world," a reference to its northern location, its ample job opportunities, and also, perhaps, to its polar winters. From November to March, frigid winds gusted off Lake Michigan, and blizzards often paralyzed the city. Strangers to this climate, blacks shivered in uninsulated, underheated frame houses not much different from the rough-planked dwellings that crowded the streets of Black Storyville.

This migrant population lived mostly on the South Side, the nation's second-largest black ghetto (after Harlem, in New York). Like the District in New Orleans, the South Side was ridden with more vice, crime, and violence than Armstrong had imagined was possible. Whereas the typical Storyville tough was part bully and part clown, content to amass a cache of fancy firearms and to guzzle more than his share of beer, criminals on the South Side operated on a bigger scale.

Armstrong with his second wife, Lil Hardin, who played the piano in Joe Oliver's Creole Jazz Band. The couple sometimes acted out playful scenes like this one onstage.

One of the most imposing underworld figures in the area was Dan Jackson, a black crime czar whose empire rested on his control of the community's prostitution and gambling. He also raked in a fortune from a new form of contraband: alcohol, whose manufacture and sale was outlawed by the 18th Amendment to the U.S. Constitution, which was ratified in 1919. On cozy terms with Chicago's powerful mayor, William "Big Bill" Thompson, Jackson tightened his grip on the South Side by making sure that blacks, in return for their votes, came in for consideration when city hall doled out funds and jobs. Such political clout was unheard of in New Orleans, where, as in most southern cities, blacks were locked out of the polling station by literacy tests, taxes, and other ruses designed to keep power in the hands of the white majority.

Chicago had its share of racism, however. In 1919, rioting claimed the lives of 23 blacks and injured 342 more, whereas 15 whites perished and another 178 suffered injury—in other words, blacks fought back. Moreover, the race riot netted immediate gains for their community. The next year, Illinois adopted a new state constitution that guaranteed civil rights to blacks.

Like many other transplanted southerners, Armstrong basked in his new situation and its practical rewards. Oliver paid his second cornetist $52 a week—enough to free Armstrong from outside employment all year round. He lived for a while in the boarding-house that Oliver found for him; then he rented an apartment.

For the first time in his life, Armstrong had ample time to practice—not that he had much catching up to do. The Creole Jazz Band played well, but its material was familiar. Oliver, who had helped hone the standard Dixieland style, saw no reason to elaborate on it. In fact, the Creole Jazz Band had forged

so definitive a sound that Armstrong's role was simply to thicken the group's texture.

In order to prevent the two cornets from getting in each other's way, Oliver decided to continue as the lead instrumentalist, with Armstrong supporting him. The only snag was the solo break, which had to be divided between two cornets. Oliver and Armstrong hit upon an ingenious scheme: duet breaks in which both men improvised at the same time, somehow producing sounds that blended together harmoniously.

Armstrong was not forced to stab blindly during his breaks. He admitted many years later, "While the rest of the band was playing, Oliver'd lean over to me and move the valves on his cornet in the notes he would play in the next breaks or a riff he'd use. So I'd play second to it. Pretty fast kid I was, in those days." Luckily, he had memorized Oliver's solo techniques and knew what to expect from the first cornet. Thus, he could focus his attention on complementing him in increasingly creative ways.

Established in 1918, Joe Oliver's Creole Jazz Band was widely considered to be the best jazz band in Chicago by the time Armstrong joined the group four years later. In this publicity photo of the band, Lil Hardin cowers as bandleader Oliver blows mightily on the cornet.

Even so, Armstrong trod lightly, careful to remain within the bounds of Oliver's rigid style. Evidence of how the band sounded survives in recordings made by the Creole Jazz Band in 1923 and 1924. These disks were the first ever made by a top-notch Dixieland band. They have been collected and reissued on albums that can be played on modern stereo systems. Despite the poor quality of the recordings, the attentive listener can sort out the various instruments well enough to be struck by how small a part Armstrong had in the Creole Jazz Band. Oliver's cornet dominates, and it is a delight to hear—restrained, melodic, and lyrical.

On occasion, however, Armstrong is allowed to solo—most memorably on "Chimes Blues" and "Froggie Moore." Today's listener is startled by the difference between Armstrong's playing and his mentor's. Oliver's sound depends heavily on his mute. Sometimes, he lodges the device inside the horn. Other times, he flaps it against the bell of the instrument, creating an effect similar to that created by the wahwah pedal that rock guitarists use.

Armstrong, by contrast, often eschews a mute altogether. More importantly, he plays with tremendous flair. Instead of merely hitting the notes, he attacks them, swinging from one pitch to the next so vigorously that the rigid structure of Dixieland seems ready to buckle. He later claimed that his playing was so much stronger than Oliver's that he stood in a distant corner of the recording studio in order not to drown him out.

Onstage at the Lincoln Gardens, Armstrong also deferred to Oliver and avoided the spotlight. This gave him a chance to drink in the surroundings of the large club, especially the motley assortment of gangsters, musicians, jazz lovers, and late-night revelers. One night when Armstrong was on the bandstand, his gaze was drawn to a puzzling sight, what he later described as "a real stout lady, with bundles in her hands, cutting across the dance floor." It was his mother! Rumors—incorrect, as it turned out—had reached Mayann that her son was ill, so she had impulsively boarded the first northbound train to Chicago.

For a few months, Armstrong shared his apartment with his mother. He escorted her around the big city and treated her, he said, to "a wardrobe with nothing but the finest—from head to foot." Mayann was so pleased with her purchases that, according to her son, "she just had to go back home to New Orleans to show all her church women the new clothes."

When his mother left, Armstrong reentered the exciting social world that Chicago offered him and other jazz artists: the cabarets, the clubs, the all-night jam sessions. His closest companion during this period was pianist Lil Hardin, who had initially eyed him askance. "Everything he had on was too small for him," she said of their first meeting. "His atrocious tie was dangling down over his protruding stomach and to top it off, he had a hairdo that called for bangs, and I do mean bangs. Bangs that jutted over his forehead like a frayed canopy." Thoroughly unimpressed by Armstrong, Lil could not understand the enthusiasm of the other New Orleans players nor why they addressed this overweight young bumpkin—riverboat meals had swollen him beyond the 220-pound mark—as "Little Louis." He was a repulsive sight to someone of her higher social station.

Lil Hardin was born in 1898, in Memphis, Tennessee. Her parents gave her many advantages, including piano lessons begun when she was a first-grader. The Hardins carefully steered their daughter away from New Orleans music—especially blues, which they regarded as music fit only for brothels and dance halls.

In 1914, Lil entered Fisk University, a black college in Nashville, Tennessee, known for its music program. She took liberal arts courses and diligently studied the classical repertory, although she secretly listed toward New Orleans music, having been introduced to it by her cousin, who played Dixieland guitar. She dropped out of Fisk in 1916 and lit out for Chicago, where her mother had moved after separating from her husband.

In Chicago, Lil landed a job at a music store owned by Richard Myknee Jones, a pianist from New Orleans. Jones seated her at a piano, where she ran through new tunes for customers interested in buying sheet music. She succeeded well enough as a "demonstrator" to earn a quick raise, from three dollars a week to eight dollars.

Jones hosted many local jazz players at his store, and Lil began jamming with them. Hooked on the new music, she auditioned for and won a spot with a combo that performed in a Chinese restaurant. Oliver soon entered the picture, forming a new band but keeping Lil as his pianist. This group evolved into the Creole Jazz Band that Armstrong joined in 1922.

Lil revised her opinion of the young cornetist once she heard him play. She was soon captivated by his talent and charmed by his shy and gentle manner. The two became lovers, intent on marriage. Lil, much worldlier than Armstrong, arranged his divorce from Daisy Parker and her own from Johnny Johnson, a struggling singer. On February 5, 1924, the pianist and cornetist were wed. Armstrong's first nuptial ceremony had been a dreary city hall affair, with no celebration and no onlookers aside from the witnesses required by law. His second, prepared by the bride, included a reception with champagne toasts and a guest list drawn from Chicago's black music world.

The new Mrs. Armstrong embarked on a mission to instill confidence in her husband. The first step was giving him big-city polish. She junked his box-back suits, marched him to a barber who shaped his hair into a more fashionable cut, and put Armstrong on a diet that eventually slimmed 50 pounds off his frame. (It was the first of many strict diets: He continued to battle a severe weight problem for the rest of his adult life.)

A thornier task was persuading Armstrong to stand up to Oliver. "Whenever Joe came to the house," Lil recalled, "you'd think that God walked in. Louis never seemed to be able to relax around him because he was so afraid of doing something that might upset him." She feared her husband's talents would be stifled as long as he settled for a secondary role to Oliver. Armstrong owed so much to his hero that he hesitated to defy him, although he finally mustered the courage to demand a regular cash salary instead of having his earnings "saved" by Oliver.

Quitting the band was a different matter. Armstrong took comfort in the protection of an older, more established musician, particularly one who jokingly referred to himself as Armstrong's stepfather. Lil pressed for her husband to leave Oliver, but Armstrong resisted.

The issue was decided, finally, by Oliver's other sidemen. They had known all along that their boss underpaid them, refusing to meet standards established by Chicago's black musicians' union. Now they learned that he cheated them as well, skimming money from their paychecks. The Dodds brothers and Honore Dutrey angrily departed, throwing the Creole Jazz Band into disarray. Armstrong, goaded by Lil, gave notice in 1924.

"You made me quit," Armstrong told his wife. "Now what do you want me to do?"

Hook up with another band, she replied.

Yet Armstrong found few takers. One bandleader, Sammy Stewart, turned him down because his skin was too dark—a form of discrimination commonly practiced by blacks against other blacks in the music world of the 1920s and 1930s. (A number of the nation's music theaters—including Harlem's prestigious Cotton Club—even barred dark-skinned blacks

Connie's Inn, one of Harlem's poshest night spots, admitted only white audiences for certain shows. Armstrong eventually headlined there and at other segregated clubs.

In the summer of 1924, Armstrong (third from left) moved to New York City after receiving an invitation from bandleader Fletcher Henderson (fifth from left) to play in his 11-piece orchestra. The large size of this group enabled it to play in big ballrooms and clubs, where more people than usual were able to hear the emerging sounds of jazz.

from the audience.) Armstrong had better luck with Ollie Powers, a singer and drummer who played regularly at the Dreamland, one of Chicago's top clubs. Powers hired Armstrong but relegated him to a minor role in his backing band.

It seemed Lil had miscalculated. The break from Oliver had yielded few rewards. But hope soon arose from an unexpected source: Fletcher Henderson and his Black Swan Troubadours, who had come a long way since passing through New Orleans in 1922. They now had a standing engagement at Roseland, a large dance hall in New York City.

Henderson's band played fizzy dance music. His arrangements were flavored by jazz, but only weakly. He longed to spiff up his sound with a hot Chicago soloist. Armstrong was his man.

Although two years had elapsed since Henderson and Armstrong first met, "I never forgot that kid," the bandleader later said. "Louis was even better than

Oliver and let no man tell you differently." Henderson contacted the cornetist and invited him to join the Black Swan Troubadours. In July 1924, Louis and Lil Armstrong packed up their belongings and moved from a great city to a greater one.

Chicago was America's top industrial center, but New York City ruled over the nation's cultural life. It had a celebrated artist's colony, Greenwich Village, with cafés and speakeasies that stayed open all night. It had Broadway, ablaze with marquees that drew customers inside plush theaters that featured dramas, musicals, and comedies. It had hundreds of clubs, cabarets, and dance halls where customers drank (illegally) and danced, sometimes to music played continuously by pairs of alternating orchestras. New York also had Harlem, the nation's prime black neighborhood. Unlike the bleak slums of New Orleans and Chicago, this uptown oasis had grand apartment buildings situated on spacious, tree-lined boulevards.

New York had everything, in short, but good jazz. It arrived in the unlikely person of Louis Armstrong, who attended his first rehearsal looking overweight and unkempt, with "high-top shoes with hooks in them, and long underwear down to his socks"—or so he was remembered by Don Redman, Henderson's gifted arranger and musical director. Evidently, Lil's remodeling had not yet taken effect.

Henderson himself was natty, trim, and reserved. A native of Atlanta, Georgia, he was raised in the same climate of respectability that had produced Lil Hardin. He even had a college degree, in chemistry.

To his credit, Henderson had no qualms about an ungainly third cornetist. He greeted Armstrong with a murmur, then handed him a musical score. Armstrong, who had not used sheet music since his riverboat days, stared wordlessly at the printed notation while his new colleagues rolled their eyes.

By now, Armstrong was used to this sort of reaction. He bided his time for a couple of weeks, meekly puzzling out his parts and delivering competent solos. Then Henderson brought in another top Chicago musician, saxophonist Buster Bailey. Armstrong was relieved to see a fellow "western" player on the stand but was piqued that Henderson felt the band needed another musician to help out on the solos. At his first Roseland gig, Bailey uncorked a solo that was hot by New York City standards. Armstrong retorted with four bars unlike anything Henderson's other musicians had ever heard.

The impact on other New York players was immediate. "I went mad with the rest of the town," trumpeter Rex Stewart later said, remembering his discovery of Armstrong. "I tried to walk like him, talk like him, eat like him, sleep like him." Armstrong soon emerged as Henderson's prize soloist—in concert and also on the many disks the band cut for various record labels.

The rise of jazz in the 1920s coincided with the emergence of New York City's Harlem as the most celebrated black community in the country. A middle-class district for blacks, it had affordable housing, tree-lined streets, and plenty of theaters, cabarets, and dance halls—ideal venues for the new music.

Featured on more than half these releases, Armstrong at last had a chance to show off his talent. He played brilliant solos on "Go 'Long Mule," "Copenhagen," "How Come You Do Me Like You Do," and, most memorably, "Sugarfoot Stomp"—Redman's rearrangement of an Oliver tune, "Dippermouth Blues" (named for Armstrong). These solos with the Fletcher Henderson Orchestra hinted at a new advance not only in Armstrong's own playing but also in the development of jazz.

For the first time in jazz history, a soloist was not satisfied merely to embroider the main melody. Instead, he used it as a springboard for sparkling inventions. He might draw out a single note, suddenly leap into a higher octave, flinging off a burst of rapid notes, then swoop back into the main melody, obediently following it yet attacking some tones and grazing others—all the while subtly playing against the regular beat, until the tune seemed bent into a different shape. Sometimes, these solos amounted only to aimless razzle-dazzle. But more often—indeed, most of the time—Armstrong constructed uniquely personal statements. And musicians and jazz fans took notice.

What especially caught their ears was Armstrong's skill as a blues player. Nearly 10 years earlier, when Armstrong was still an apprentice, Mutt Carey had marveled at his feeling for the blues. At that time, the blues was still a folk form limited to the South. Tunes were not written down; they were sung, and evolved like jokes, changed and elaborated in the retelling. Then, in 1914, W. C. Handy, a black composer in Memphis, Tennessee, wrote and published "St. Louis Blues." It caused a national sensation and was even performed by white singers, such as vaudeville star Sophie Tucker.

Gradually, blues seeped into mainstream music. One reason was the rising interest in black culture,

Among the main characteristics of the Harlem Renaissance was an unabashed celebration of black life. The blithe spirit of jazz, which emerged as the period's representative sound, is depicted in this 1927 watercolor by Palmer Hayden.

much of it centered in New York City, the cradle of the Harlem Renaissance. During this glorious epoch, many black artists fashioned memorable works richly spiced with the ingredients of black folklore. Their art often celebrated the blues as the purest expression of the black experience in America. For the first time, "race" music caught on with audiences of every description, and it opened many doors for black performers, especially three female vocalists: Clara Smith, Gertrude "Ma" Rainey, and Bessie Smith.

At the apex of this elite trio stood Bessie Smith. She was born in Chattanooga, Tennessee, in 1893. As a child, she sang on street corners, as Armstrong himself had done. In about 1910, Smith came under the tutelage of Ma Rainey and joined her road show, which toured through the South, entertaining black audiences in theaters and tent shows.

Smith had amassed a regional following by the time the blues came into vogue. In 1923, Columbia Records invited her to New York City. There she cut "Down Hearted Blues." This tune had already been recorded by several artists, but Smith's version was so original—so powerful in its sorrow—that within 6 months it sold 780,000 copies, an astronomical total for the time.

In January 1925, Armstrong was asked to team with Smith on five blues recordings. It was a big break that he gladly accepted. Because Smith was a national sensation and he was a relative unknown, his task was to back her up, complementing her vocals with subdued playing (a third musician, Fred Longshaw, a pianist and organist, rounded out the sessions). This pairing of Smith and Armstrong was inspired. Both were highly talented and both were prodigious improvisers.

Armstrong later described how the sessions worked. On the appointed day, Smith appeared at the studio with "the words and tune in her head, and we'd just run it down once. Then she'd sing a few lines, and I'd play something to fill it in, and some nice, beautiful notes behind her." The high points of the sessions were "You've Been a Good Ole Wagon," "Sobbin' Hearted Blues," and a magnificent version of Handy's "St. Louis Blues." Recordings of these songs are still available today, and listeners can hear for themselves why Armstrong said of his work with Bessie Smith, "Everything I did with her I *like*."

Smith received $3,000 for a recording session at the height of her success. Armstrong, who was only six years her junior, wondered if the moment would ever come when he, too, would break outside the orbit of jazz and become nationally known.

Blues singer Bessie Smith is featured on the sheet-music cover of "Chirpin' the Blues," one of the many tunes that she helped popularize. In 1925—at the height of her success—she made a series of recordings with Armstrong backing her vocals on his cornet.

A glimmer of recognition finally appeared in April 1925, when *New York Age*, a black newspaper, published an article that rated the Black Swan Troubadours among the top three bands in the country and featured a list of the band's personnel. Yet it was not exactly the kind of acknowledgment Henderson's cornetist was looking for. His name was misspelled as "Lewis Armstrong."

By late 1925, Armstrong had grown disenchanted with the Black Swan Troubadours. Their playing had fallen off, in part because Henderson, an erratic leader, failed to discipline his players. Some of them—saxophonists Buster Bailey and Coleman Hawkins and trumpeter Joe Smith—seemed committed to music. But others, seduced by success, caroused late into the night. Often, as Armstrong once complained to an interviewer, they would "come out on the stand and goof, wouldn't keep time, didn't hit notes on time—and figured 'so what?' I didn't appreciate that. I was always serious about my music."

Armstrong was also irked by another matter. Henderson took a dim view of the cornetist's singing. Ever since Armstrong had joined the quartet that worked the streets of Storyville, he had loved to vocalize. He had found occasion to do it in the New Orleans honky-tonks and clubs, and later with the Creole Jazz Band, though not on any of the recordings that survive from the Chicago sessions. But Henderson, who raised no objection when lesser musicians got stewed to the gills, adamantly refused to indulge his star's singing, even after Armstrong wowed a Roseland audience during an amateur night with his rendition of a hit tune, "Everybody Loves My Baby, But My Baby Don't Love Nobody But Me."

Armstrong did not merely enjoy singing; he realized that it might hold the key to any future success. He need only reflect on the huge sums Bessie Smith pocketed for her recording sessions compared with the $50 or $100 paid to him, her peer as a musician. If he wanted to sing, he would have to break away from Henderson, just as he had broken away from Oliver in order to establish himself as a solo cornetist. The second move was easier to make. He owed a good deal to Henderson, but not nearly as much as he had to Oliver.

There was another reason to leave Henderson: Lil. She had returned to Chicago early in the year to care for her ailing mother. A lonely Armstrong had subsequently taken up with a New York woman, and word of the relationship reached Lil in Chicago. She wanted her husband beside her and issued an ultimatum. Either he returned to Chicago or their marriage was off.

Lil sweetened her threat with some welcome news. She had put together a band of her own at the Dreamland, and the owner of the club, Bill Bottoms, had agreed to pay her husband $75 a week to be the band's main attraction.

Once again, Armstrong displayed faultless timing. He had learned to play the cornet at the precise moment when the Dixieland sound leapt full-grown

By the time Armstrong returned to Chicago in late 1925, his reputation had grown to such an extent that he was able to head his own orchestra. He is shown here one year later with Louis Armstrong and His Stompers, which included his friends Zutty Singleton on drums and Earl Hines on piano.

from the streets of Storyville. He had ventured north to join the Creole Jazz Band at the peak of King Oliver's reign. He had arrived in New York just when the city was starved for a hot soloist. And now he was returning to Chicago, still the mecca of the new music, just as the nation was entering the Jazz Age.

In New York, Armstrong's reputation was limited to the music industry—the insular world of recording studios, musicians, and ardent fans. But in Chicago, the arrival of Louis Armstrong was general news. On November 7, 1925, the *Chicago Defender*, the city's leading black publication, announced that "Mr. Armstrong, the famous cornetist, will grace the first chair in the Dreamland Orchestra sometime this week." It seemed inevitable that Armstrong would step to the fore of the Chicago scene.

It happened almost instantaneously. A week after Armstrong's return, executives at OKeh Records invited him in for a recording session. He brought along Lil and some old pals: clarinetist Johnny Dodds; trombonist Kid Ory, up from New Orleans and part of Oliver's new band; banjoist Johnny St. Cyr; and drummer Baby Dodds, Johnny's younger brother. Because of Armstrong's reputation as a soloist, the group recorded under his name, styling themselves Louis Armstrong and His Hot Five. Placed at the head of this talented crew, Armstrong switched from the cornet to the more powerful trumpet.

No doubt the other New Orleans hands felt a twinge of envy at the top billing given Joe Oliver's former sidekick. But Armstrong took his new status in stride. Inside the studio, he refused to put on airs; instead, he treated his colleagues as equals, according to Ory. After the band cut a side, the trombonist recalled, "Louis would say, 'Was that all right?' And if one of us thought we could do it over and do it better, why Louis would tell [the engineer] we wanted to do it again, and so we would do it over."

During the next three years, Armstrong recorded more than 50 songs with this group and with different variations of it: Louis Armstrong and His Hot Seven, Louis Armstrong and His Orchestra, Louis Armstrong and His Savoy Ballroom Five, Louis Armstrong and His Hot Four. The personnel underwent revision—one of the changes saw Lil replaced by Earl "Fatha" Hines, among the top artists of the day—and the group's style of play evolved from session to session. Taken together, these recordings—known collectively as the Hot Five sessions—remain among the high points of jazz. Whereas Armstrong's solo work with Fletcher Henderson and Bessie Smith had sent forth ripples of genius, his playing in the Hot Five sessions gathered the force of a tidal wave.

On these cuts, Armstrong ranged all over the jazz map. He produced a hit single, "Heebie Jeebies," whose nonsense scat lines caused a sensation. He refurbished Dixieland standards—"Muskrat Ramble," "Willie the Weeper"—with blistering solos. He tenderly probed the depths of sorrow with his blues vocal on "St. James Infirmary." He lifted improvisation onto a plane of rare artistry in "Potato Head." The highlight of the sessions was, of course, "West End Blues," with its brilliant solo interplay that intoned the end of Dixieland and heralded the birth of a new jazz era.

Sales figures alone did not measure the impact of the Hot Five recordings. They did well, but nowhere near as well as, say, Bessie Smith's blues disks. Nor did these sessions instantly sweep Armstrong into the popular mainstream. Only a handful of the tracks featured his vocals; fewer still recycled the hit tunes that most audiences preferred. To a number of listeners, in fact, the music played by Arsmtrong and the Hot Five seemed difficult and inaccessible.

But others responded to the Hot Five sessions with a delight that verged on passion, and Armstrong sud-

A publicity photo of Armstrong's Hot Five, a group that played together from November 1925 to December 1928. Pianist Lil Hardin (right) eventually gave up her spot in the group to Earl Hines, one of the few soloists of the time who could hold his own with Armstrong.

denly found himself in demand all over the city. "Things were jumping so around Chicago at that time," he fondly recalled. "There was more work than a cat could shake a stick at."

Armstrong played at the Dreamland with Lil's band and also at the Vendome Theatre, where he sat in with an orchestra that supplied background music for silent movies and stage acts. He then sped to one of a number of integrated clubs—called black-and-tans—and played until dawn, when he trekked to the OKeh studio or to jam sessions. It was a schedule as exhausting as the one he had kept in New Orleans, when he worked the coal wagon all day long, then rang in the dawn at the honky-tonks.

Success had come, and with it came new pressures. Audiences now insisted he climb out of the orchestra pit and onto the stage. Armstrong was reluctant to oblige them. Years later, he explained why: "If I'd gotten up there on that stage, people would say, 'Shoot, he just wants to be a star, an individual,' and even your own musicians you're playing with won't [treat you with] that same warmth."

In the end, however, Armstrong lunged after stardom. At the same time that he made the Hot Five recordings, he began the process of transforming himself into a crowd-pleasing entertainer. He might still be shy, he might fear the resentment of other musicians, but he relished the hushed anticipation and the tense fidgeting at 100 tables as he lifted his horn to his lips and blew the first golden notes. Warmed by constant applause, he honed his act to suit the expectations of his fans.

Audiences especially delighted in Armstrong's singing. He did not have a pretty voice. In fact, he rasped. But he had an uncanny knack for landing squarely in the middle of every note, and his vocal style was lit with the same spontaneity that shone through his trumpet solos. Armstrong did not merely sing—he growled, spoke, and tossed off complex scat lines the way a motor tosses sparks. He effortlessly turned melodies into his personal property and pointed the way for the expressive exaggerations of later vocalists such as Fats Waller, Billie Holiday, and even Bob Dylan.

Armstrong also enlivened his stage act with gags and jokes similar to those perfected by the vaudeville and silent comedy stars so popular at the time. Nor was he above clownish mugging, something white audiences expected of black performers. He grinned from ear to ear, rolled his eyes, whined like a plantation slave, or droned like a pompous preacher. He hatched a bit of vaudeville foolery with his drummer, Zutty Singleton, who "would dress up as one of those real loud and rough gals, with a short skirt, and a pillow in back of him," Armstrong said. "I was dressed in old rags, the beak of my cap turned around like a tough guy and [Zutty] was my gal. As he would come down the aisle, interrupting my song, the people would just scream with laughter."

Jazz purists groaned at Armstrong's clowning but found solace in the recordings he continued to make with the Hot Five: miracles of daring, sophistication, and subtlety. By the late 1920s, he had become one of those rare artists whom ordinary categories cannot contain. He was two people: a jazz explorer who energetically pressed his medium to new limits, and an entertainer who delighted audiences out for a night of good cheer. Small wonder that he once said, "All in all, the twenties in Chicago were some of my finest days."

For Armstrong, this time was not free of sadness, however. In 1927, during one of her trips to Chicago, Mayann Armstrong died. The cause was never determined, although hard living—including heavy drinking—took its toll. Her son, who paid for an elaborate funeral, was overcome with grief. "Probably the only time I ever cried [was] when they put that cover over her face," he said. Mayann's life had been troubled, but she died knowing her son had become a success.

In 1928, hard times hit the Chicago music scene. Since 1919, when Prohibition made alcohol contraband, the city had been sliding into corruption. Bootlegging had become a lucrative and dangerous business, similar to drug trafficking today. Gangland slayings— a common occurrence—went unpunished, even when they claimed the lives of innocent bystanders.

Matters had gotten so bad that some private citizens formed the Chicago Crime Commission and

began an investigation into the ties between mob leaders such as Al Capone and Dion O'Bannion and local politicians such as Mayor Bill Thompson. The commission passed its findings on to local newspapers, and scandal soon engulfed the city. In the 1928 Democratic primary, Thompson was outpolled by a reform candidate, and a huge campaign ensued to clean up Chicago.

The first order of business was flushing the city dry of alcohol. Police staged massive raids on clubs and speakeasies, which were forced to close their doors. Hundreds of jazz players subsequently lost their jobs. Those from New Orleans recalled the events of 1917, when the prostitution ban shut down Storyville.

The Chicago scene had turned bleak, but the rest of the nation was still in the mood for entertainment, and Armstrong had emerged as someone who could deliver it. No one knew this better than Tommy Rockwell, a record producer who had been recording Armstrong's work for the past two years. In 1929, Rockwell branched out into management. He signed Armstrong to a contract, then brought him to New York City, booking an engagement for him at the

Armstrong and Zutty Singleton (second from left) before their careers diverged in 1929. When the two were offstage, the bandleader usually took a backseat to his assertive friend.

Savoy, a large ballroom in Harlem. Armstrong arrived from Chicago with a backing band led by pianist Luis Russell, an alumnus of one of Oliver's combos.

Armstrong's growing fame was apparent on the night of the show. Fans mobbed the sidewalks outside the Savoy; thousands had to be turned away. After the engagement, he stayed on in New York to attend a number of banquets held in his honor. Many people in the music industry showed up, including some top white musicians.

One of these fetes lasted until dawn, when Rockwell gathered up a handful of the best players in the room—white and black—in order to put together an impromptu recording session. Fortified by a 6:00 A.M. breakfast and a gallon of whiskey, the men trouped to OKeh's New York studio for one of the first integrated recording dates in jazz history. Armstrong, the key performer, served up a delectable vocal on "I Can't Give You Anything but Love," a popular Broadway tune, and delivered a scorching trumpet solo on "Mahogany Hall Stomp."

In 1929, Armstrong returned to Chicago, where more gigs awaited him, including a feature appearance at the Regal Theatre. Rockwell, inspired by his client's fruitful sojourn in New York City, scouted around for more work there and struck up a deal with Vincent Youmans, a Broadway composer who had drafted several songs for a show, *Great Day*, that would use an integrated cast and a black orchestra led by Fletcher Henderson. Rockwell secured a spot in the pit for Armstrong.

The trumpeter headed for New York in May along with Carroll Dickerson's orchestra, which had been struggling to get work in Chicago. The entourage "piled into about four dilapidated cars," according to Armstrong, including his own '28 Hupmobile, purchased with the proceeds from a book of trumpet exercises he had prepared for a music publisher. Arm-

To help finance his return to New York City in 1929 after the Chicago music scene turned bleak, Armstrong prepared an exercise book, Louis Armstrong's 50 Hot Choruses for Cornet. He had used similar works when he was in his teens.

strong put Zutty Singleton behind the wheel and slept in the back seat during the trip East. "On our way we went sightseeing," the star recalled, "stopping in a lot of towns where they had been listening to us over the radio from the Savoy in Chicago. They treated us royally. Our money was no good." It was a lucky break because each of the men carried only a $20 stipend scraped together by Armstrong.

After detouring through Buffalo and Niagara Falls, the group arrived in New York City wedged tightly into the two autos that survived the trip. The Hupmobile wheezed over the last miles, and when it reached

Pianist and vocalist Thomas "Fats" Waller composed several hit songs for the wildly successful musical revue Hot Chocolates, *which opened in Harlem in May 1929. Armstrong was added to the show's cast as a featured performer one month later, when it moved to Broadway.*

Times Square—where Broadway meets 42nd Street— the radiator cap shot off loudly. A police officer, suspicious of the car's Illinois license plates and its crowded cargo of black men, inspected the vehicle for firearms.

The entourage received an even colder reception from Armstrong's manager. Rockwell had summoned only the star, not his backing band, and he groused about being burdened with a dozen unemployed musicians. Armstrong would not dismiss them, however, and he found work with them the next night as unannounced performers at the Audubon Theater, a black hall, standing in for the overbooked Duke Ellington and His Orchestra. Zutty Singleton later remembered that "the pit band looked pretty surprised when the curtain went up and there we were on stage." Unfazed, Armstrong sailed into the opening bars of "St. Louis Blues." When he finished, Singleton recalled, "even the band in the pit stood up and applauded for him."

Things went less smoothly at the Youmans show. A white conductor took over preparations for the *Great Day* orchestra and began dismissing the black musicians. Fletcher Henderson stood idly by, failing once again to assert himself. This time the consequences proved disastrous: Some of the men vowed never to play with him again. There was one small consolation: *Great Day* flopped.

As the vogue for black music raged on, Armstrong reaped its benefits, including a second shot at Broadway. *Hot Chocolates*, a black musical revue, opened in June 1929 with Armstrong in the orchestra pit. Audiences and critics raved when he sang "Ain't Misbehavin'," which has since become a classic, and it was not long before he climbed out of the pit and onto the stage. He was added to the cast of another song, "A Thousand Pounds of Rhythm," forming a beefy trio with the review's composer, Thomas "Fats"

Waller—one of the great jazz pianists of the era—
and the female lead, Edith Wilson. *Hot Chocolates*
did so well—running for 219 nights—that a version
of it was also staged at a sleek Harlem club, Connie's
Inn, where Armstrong reprised his Broadway act for
integrated audiences.

Offers for the 30-year-old musician started to pour
into Tommy Rockwell's office. The agent booked
Armstrong for a third June engagement, fronting the
Carroll Dickerson band at the Lafayette Theatre. At
OKeh sessions, Armstrong effortlessly laid down a
mix of songs, including his hits from *Hot Chocolates*.
In July, he was feted by white jazz artists, who presented him with an engraved watch: "To Louis Armstrong, World's Greatest Cornetist, from the Musicians
of New York."

In Chicago, Armstrong the showman had happily
coexisted with Armstrong the artist. But now a con-
flict arose between them, instigated by Rockwell. He

The revue Hot Chocolates *featured a dozen dancers whose stage
name gave the show its title.
Every night after they concluded
their act on Broadway, they
would commute to Harlem with
the other performers and reprise
much of the show at Connie's
Inn.*

badgered Armstrong to dismiss the Dickerson band and to perform instead with his own clients, the Luis Russell Orchestra. Rockwell argued that the Dickerson men were not cut out for big-time entertainment and would hold Armstrong back. Lil Armstrong agreed. The star himself demurred. He liked playing with the Dickerson men, and many, such as Zutty Singleton, were trusted friends.

Finally, Armstrong caved in. The news of their dismissal crushed the Dickerson band. Their future had been riding on the success of their leader. Without him, most were lost—but not Zutty Singleton, a deft drummer avidly sought by other bands. He patiently waited for an offer to continue with Armstrong.

When no word came, Singleton forced the issue, paying a call on Armstrong. "I asked Louis did he want me to stay with him?" the drummer later recalled. "Because if not I've got a job to stay in Connie's Inn. . . . And so Louis told me how much money he had a chance to make and everything like that. And that's when I told Louis . . . friendship is one thing and business is another." Things had changed since 1922, when Armstrong refused to join the Black Swan Troubadours unless Singleton was invited, too.

To Singleton and the others, it seemed that Armstrong had been spoiled by success. But Armstrong's actions were not really out of character. Since his days in the Waifs' Home, he had taken pains to further his career. He had withstood the menacing scowls of Peter Davis, had annihilated the doubts of hostile colleagues in Kid Ory's band, had met the challenges posed by Fate Marable, had broken with Oliver, and had quit the security of the Fletcher Henderson Orchestra.

Nonetheless, this latest move indicated that Armstrong had reached a new plateau. Previously, he had always favored familiar company. He had turned

down Henderson's first offer because it did not include Singleton. Loyalty again caused him to return to New York with a carful of buddies, determined to find work for them all. He now wanted to go it alone and to shed all ties with his past.

What was the reason? *Hot Chocolates*. Before joining its cast, Armstrong had known success, but he had not managed to rise above the seamy milieu of speakeasies and dance halls. And as much as the music world might laud his gifts, he still seemed likely to spend most of his nights in such places, serving up "race music" for thugs, prostitutes, and other assorted "nightlifers," many of them pickled on bathtub gin.

Broadway offered something different: plush seats, uniformed ushers, mannerly audiences gripping printed programs. Broadway signaled the beginning of respectability, and to Armstrong it was a much greater prize than critical acclaim. Yet stardom, he would learn soon enough, had drawbacks of its own. In the next decade, Armstrong, jazz, and the entire nation would suffer hard times. ◖◗

A star by the late 1920s, Armstrong felt uneasy at first when it came to posing front and center while his colleagues retreated from the spotlight. "Forget all the . . . critics, the musicians," he was advised by Joe Glaser, one of his managers. "Play for the public. Sing and play and smile."

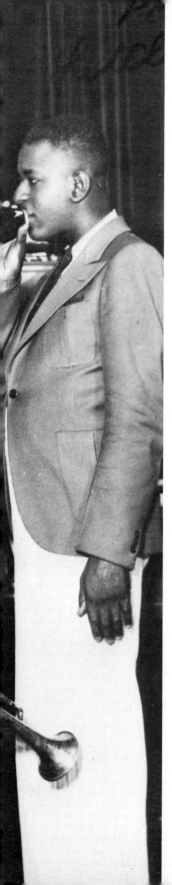

7

HIGHS AND LOWS

❦

O N OCTOBER 29, 1929, the New York Stock Exchange crashed, and the American economy tumbled with it, bringing the gaudy spree and upbeat mood of the 1920s to an end. The country immediately fell into a great economic depression. Within 3 years, more than 5,000 American banks lost all their capital, countless businesses skidded into bankruptcy, and millions of citizens, bereft of work and savings, shivered on breadlines. The hardest hit of all were blacks, most of whom slid deeper into poverty. Even Harlem, robbed of its glitter, decayed into a slum.

The music industry also took a drubbing. Record sales slumped, theaters and nightclubs closed, and skilled performers desperately competed for low-paying gigs. Marginal players, such as the Dickerson sidemen, drifted out of New York and out of music.

Big stars, too, fell by the wayside. One was Bessie Smith, whose melancholy blues dropped out of fashion—audiences now thirsted for lighthearted cheer. She tried widening her repertory to include happier tunes, but they failed to catch on.

More versatile performers fared better. One such was Armstrong. Egged on by Tommy Rockwell and by Victor—his new record company—he continued

Armstrong (bottom right) made his first return trip to New Orleans in 1931 as part of a nationwide tour. He remained in his hometown for several months, performing at the Suburban Gardens (shown here), a lavish night spot that admitted only whites.

to purge his act of blues and jazz and to add sugary love songs and humorous novelty tunes. In the studio and onstage, he sang more than he trumpeted, and when he picked up his horn it was to regale audiences with grandstanding rather than with subtle improvisation. He abandoned small Dixieland-style ensembles and instead fronted large bands with a dozen or more instruments.

A typical Armstrong disk made in the early 1930s began with a simple trumpet solo that straightforwardly introduced the main melody. Next, he sang a few choruses in his patented raspy style, ad-libbing new lyrics and tossing in nifty scat phrases. He then rested while the band lumbered through a few bars. He concluded with a flurry of fancy horn playing bunched with high notes. The new formula paid off. In 1930, he embarked on a nationwide tour, playing clubs and dance halls in Philadelphia, Washington, D.C., Chicago, San Francisco, and Los Angeles.

Armstrong's reputation was not limited to the United States. Jazz was gaining popularity in Europe, where record companies imported American hits. Since the late 1920s, Parlophone, an English label, had been releasing Armstrong disks, including some recorded with the Hot Five. Interest grew, and in 1932, Armstrong voyaged across the ocean to headline for two weeks at the Palladium, a London concert hall. Tremendous hoopla greeted his arrival. *Melody Maker*, the country's top jazz magazine, delayed publication for a day in order to run a feature story on the "Colored Trumpet King."

Backed by American musicians rushed over to England from Paris, Armstrong opened before a full house. The audience was prepared for spectacular playing but not for a high-voltage stage act. *Melody Maker*'s reviewer marveled that Armstrong "puts enough energy in his half-hour's performance to last the average man several years."

The next stop for Armstrong was Paris, where his show thrilled the city's fervent jazz coterie. He sailed home in November with an international reputation and a new nickname. Onstage, Armstrong often referred to himself as *Satchelmouth*, a reference—like *Dippermouth*—to his enormous grin. A British journalist covering the tour was thrown by Armstrong's Southern accent. Instead of *Satchelmouth* he heard *Satchmo*, and the new version stuck.

Back home, Armstrong was constantly on the go. The rare performer who preferred one-night gigs to longer engagements, he gladly appeared wherever he was wanted. Lil, however, wearied of touring—the grim succession of segregated hotels, the clothes wrinkling in suitcases, the meals grabbed on the run, the hours spent jouncing along bumpy highways in a bus filled with snoozing musicians.

Traveling was not Lil's only complaint. For years she had tolerated her husband's infidelities, but her patience had steadily been wearing thin since 1928,

In 1932, Armstrong launched his first European tour at the Palladium (shown here) in London. After his opening-night show, Melody Maker magazine reported that Armstrong was "a unique phenomenon, an electric personality—easily the greatest America has sent us so far."

when he began a relationship with Alpha Smith, a maid employed by a wealthy Chicago family. By 1931, when the affair gave no signs of cooling, Lil was fed up. "You don't need me now [that] you're earning $1,000 a week," she told her husband. "Let's call it a day."

In parting, Armstrong was generous, turning over to Lil the house they owned in Chicago, along with most of his savings. The two remained on good terms. Indeed, Lil wore Armstrong's wedding ring until 1971, when she died at the piano during a memorial concert for her former husband.

Other hurts did not mend. In the early 1930s, Armstrong began to suffer mouth ailments. Thousands of hours in the studio and onstage had left him with painful calluses. Armstrong rarely sought medical help, preferring home remedies. Some were harmless, such as coating his lips with balm. Others were dangerous, such as slicing off the hardened tissue with a razor.

Armstrong's lip trouble was aggravated by managers who booked him night after night, not allowing him any rest. The worst offender was Johnny Collins, whom Armstrong—for unclear reasons—signed with in 1931, replacing Tommy Rockwell, who had served him fairly well. Both Rockwell and Collins had mob connections, and Armstrong became the prize in a tug-of-war that was part nightmare, part farce.

The struggle began after Collins fixed up Armstrong with a backing band and booked the act into a swanky Chicago club. The star was relaxing in his dressing room on opening night when a tough-looking man barged in and, as Armstrong later said, proceeded "to instruct me that I will open in such-and-such a club in New York the next night. I tell him I got this Chicago engagement and don't plan no traveling. Then I hear this sound: SNAP! CLICK! I turn around and he has pulled this vast revolver on me and cocked it." Armstrong muddled through his show, then sneaked out of town, joining his sidemen on a train bound for Louisville, Kentucky, where they easily landed a gig.

Thus, stardom, which Armstrong had hoped would vault him out of the dank underbelly of the music world, pitched him further into it. Collins and Rockwell saw Armstrong as a ticket to riches, and both were loath to relinquish him. During the next few years, their war escalated so intensively that Armstrong could not safely perform in Chicago or New York. In fact, one reason that he accepted the offer to play in London was to escape.

As troublesome as Rockwell could be, he at least knew something about the music industry. Collins, however, wore his ignorance like a badge. He nearly botched Armstrong's first European trip by waiting until the last minute to find a backing band, leaving Armstrong little time to rehearse. He even neglected to reserve a hotel room for his client. Furthermore, Collins drank heavily, ran up huge tabs that he refused to pay, and abused promoters, journalists, and whoever else stumbled into his path. Back in the United States, he drove Armstrong like a dray horse, loading him up with studio and concert dates when it was apparent that the star's mouth was causing him severe pain and that he was on the brink of collapse.

Armstrong did not protest until his second trip abroad, in the summer of 1933, when he discovered that his taxes had gone unpaid by his manager, who had also neglected to send money to Lil, as he had been asked to do. Armstrong promptly fired Collins, who stayed on to collect every last cent owed him from the contracts he had signed.

A new manager, Englishman Jack Hylton, stepped into the breach, and matters improved overnight. Hylton booked gigs in England, Holland, and Denmark, but he also scheduled periods of rest and recuperation. A musician himself—in fact, he was Europe's best bandleader—Hylton took Armstrong

Armstrong and companion Alpha Smith in 1933, during his second European tour. After a 10-year courtship, in 1938 she became his third wife.

seriously as an artist. He urged his client to play legitimate jazz rather than tuneful corn and to cut down on his mugging. This was precisely the sort of management Armstrong needed. His lip healed, his spirits soared, and he even considered settling permanently in London.

But it was not to be. New conflicts surfaced in 1934, when another American jazz giant landed in England: saxophonist Coleman Hawkins, whom Armstrong had played with in the Fletcher Henderson Orchestra. Hawkins had since become a star soloist in his own right, and his arrival in Europe seemed the ideal opportunity for Armstrong to team up with a musician of his own caliber. Hylton organized some concerts, but at the last minute Armstrong bowed out because he had misgivings about sharing the limelight.

Armstrong broke with Hylton, headed for Paris, and put together a band composed of American expatriates. A French manager, N. J. Canetti, booked him in local clubs and at a recording studio, then set

Joe Glaser (second from left) was a rarity among whites: a manager who went on the road with black bands. Armstrong (fourth from left) was also a rarity: a star who joined his sidemen on the bus rather than ride in a separate vehicle.

up a long tour through France, Italy, and Switzerland. Halfway through, Armstrong withdrew, citing problems with his lip. Canetti, left high and dry, sued his client. Armstrong sued in return, then voyaged back to the United States.

In America, Armstrong struggled back to his feet. First, he found a new manager, Joe Glaser, a Chicago native who was about the same age as Armstrong but came from a considerably different background. For one thing, he was Jewish. For another, his father was a doctor who had hoped his son would follow in his footsteps. But Glaser had other plans. In his teens, he had deserted the middle-class environment in which he had been raised and began to haunt the Chicago night world of gamblers, bootleggers, and mobsters. In the 1920s, he owned a car dealership, managed some prizefighters, and headed a prostitution ring— all mob-related enterprises and thus ripe for ruin in 1928, when the Chicago Crime Commission began its crusade. By 1935, Glaser was looking to salvage his finances.

So was Armstrong. He had returned from Europe chased by a lawsuit. He owed alimony to Lil and taxes to the Internal Revenue Service, and Johnny Collins and Tommy Rockwell still panted after him. And during nearly two years abroad, he had made no recordings for Victor and had not appeared on an American stage. To top it off, a doctor warned him not to play the trumpet for six months while his battered lip healed. His career had run aground. "I couldn't go no further with all them shysters yiping at me," he said. "Everything was in hock. Had a 32-hundred dollar Buick. . . . Sold it for $300. I decided Joe Glaser was going to be my manager; had always admired the way he treat[ed] his help. . . . So we signed up."

It was one of the wisest decisions Armstrong ever made. Glaser, just as tough as Rockwell and Collins, was smarter, more energetic, and better organized.

He dealt with Armstrong's bills and taxes, and thoroughly planned his performances and studio sessions.

One of Glaser's first moves as Armstrong's manager was to buy out Johnny Collins, who still had contractual claims to Armstrong. At last the star was free to perform in top clubs. Next, Glaser assembled a backing band for Armstrong and booked a tour in July 1935 that included a stop at the Apollo Theatre in Harlem and similar large halls—much better places than the tawdry dance halls Collins had favored. Unlike many white managers, Glaser traveled with the band, standing up for his client when trouble arose on the road—with hostile police, crooked club owners, and shifty bus-rental agents. Glaser also negotiated a recording contract with a new company, Decca. In short order, Armstrong's affairs were in good shape.

An ambitious man, Glaser set about promoting his star to white audiences, who responded enthusiastically. The October 1935 issue of *Esquire* magazine, then in its infancy, featured a whimsical cartoon—racist by today's standards—depicting Armstrong's development as a trumpeter. A month later, a full-page photo of Armstrong ran in *Vanity Fair*, a fashionable magazine that covered society and the arts.

Hollywood beckoned, too. The movie studios had switched from silent films to "talkies" in 1927, when vaudeville star Al Jolson broke box office records with his vocals in *The Jazz Singer*. Armstrong made his own screen debut in 1930, singing and trumpeting in an otherwise forgotten film, *Ex: Flame*. Under Glaser's management, more offers came.

Armstrong emerged as a popular draw, the first black ever to be offered steady work in high-budget Hollywood productions. In 1936, he landed a cameo role in *Pennies from Heaven*, which starred crooner Bing Crosby. Armstrong's rendition of the title track became a hit. The next year, he appeared in *Artists*

Although Armstrong became a popular draw in Hollywood movies—he appeared in more than 25 films—he was usually relegated to cameo roles that played on crude racial stereotypes of the obliging black. He is shown here grinning for the camera in the 1936 film Pennies from Heaven.

and Models, and in 1938 he was in *Every Day's a Holiday,* a vehicle for Mae West, one of the top comic stars of the decade.

Another major medium was radio, especially after the depression cut record sales. Like today's television programs, radio shows were financed by commercial sponsors, and they often resisted having their products associated with blacks. But Glaser cultivated good connections with radio programmers and prodded them to open their microphones to Armstrong, who played a crucial role in integrating the airwaves.

By the end of the 1930s, Armstrong ranked among the best-known blacks in America, a pioneer who had made headway into areas of show business usually limited to whites. He was a modest pathbreaker, however. He seldom made an issue of race, despite the grave indignities he routinely suffered. Like all black performers, he was rarely allowed to sleep in good hotels or to dine in choice restaurants, although he often entertained there, giving pleasure to the same people who casually banished him to crosstown slums when his show ended.

The double standard was especially blatant in the South, where Jim Crow laws remained on the books. A typical incident occurred in 1931, when Armstrong made a southern tour that included a homecoming engagement in New Orleans. Citizens—black and white—thronged the railroad station. Bands blared and banners flapped. But when the star arrived for his gig at a segregated restaurant, the radio announcer—the concert was broadcast live—refused to introduce the black performer. Armstrong was forced to introduce himself.

Armstrong was also sobered by the hard luck that had bruised some of the top names in music. Bessie Smith was soon joined in obscurity by Joe Oliver. The King's troubles had begun in the mid-1920s, when, lulled by his success in Chicago, he had turned down offers to take his act to New York City, where most top performers migrated. He finally went there in 1927, but he unwisely snubbed the Cotton Club because the pay was too low. Other employers shied away, and Oliver's band dissolved.

An avid baseball fan, Armstrong (far right) outfitted a team, the "Secret 9," during his stay in New Orleans in 1931. The ball club competed against other all-black squads in the Negro Leagues, which gave blacks, barred at the time from the major leagues, their only opportunity to play professional baseball.

The King could not be blamed for his other troubles. In 1926, he contracted pyorrhea, a gum ailment that gradually loosens the teeth. By 1928, his gums had weakened so badly that he could no longer press his upper lip against his cornet. He was fitted with dentures, but they enabled him to play only at half force and with severe discomfort. He subsequently turned over most of his solos to sidemen.

Soon, the Great Depression arrived, and recording companies began trimming their rosters. Oliver's contract with Victor came up for renewal in 1931, and the company let him go. Oliver was cornered. He could not record, he was locked out of New York, and Chicago had been slammed shut by the Citizens Crime Commission. His only option was to go on the road.

Oliver scraped together a band, rented a dowdy bus, and toured the South, sticking to small towns because he could not bear making a downtrodden appearance in cities—including New Orleans—where the Oliver name still meant something. Again, his pride cost him. Small-time bookings meant measly paychecks, bad meals, wretched lodging, and unsafe transportation. After their bus broke down on a freezing highway, many sidemen deserted Oliver. The rest were then fleeced by an agent who left them so broke they had to travel home in a coal truck.

Eventually, Oliver gave up performing and drifted into menial jobs. One was as a janitor in a billiard parlor. "I open the pool rooms at 9 A.M. and close at 12 midnite," Oliver wrote to his sister in 1937, when he still dreamed of forming a new band. "If the money was only as much as the hours I'd be all set." In truth, he could not even muster three dollars for blood-pressure treatments.

Armstrong had observed his hero's decline from afar and had periodically sent him money. In 1937, he paid Oliver a visit in Savannah, Georgia, when

a gig brought him there. Oliver, Armstrong maintained, was "so bad off and broke, he [was forced to
run] a little vegetable stand selling tomatoes and po-
tatoes. He was standing there in his shirtsleeves. No
tears. Just glad to see us. Just another day. He had
that spirit."

Buoyed by this reunion, Oliver started up a kitty
that he hoped would finance his comeback. "Got
$1.60 in it and won't touch it," he vowed in one of
his last letters. "I'm going to try and save myself a
ticket to New York."

He never made it. On April 10, 1938, Oliver
died of a cerebral hemorrhage. The New York City
musicians' union paid for his body to be shipped north
and buried in a Bronx cemetery. Twenty-one years
earlier, Armstrong had joined the New Orleans throng
that saw Oliver off to Chicago. Now he was among
those who bade a final farewell to the King at his
funeral in New York City.

Unlike Oliver, whose reign had never been secure, Armstrong showed no signs of faltering. He
remained the top trumpeter in jazz, unrivaled for his
technical prowess and wealth of musical ideas. He
was even better known as a vocalist, stamping his
unmistakable imprint on commercial hits: "I'm in the
Mood for Love," "Sweethearts on Parade," "Red Sails
in the Sunset," and many others. Armstrong himself
credited his widening appeal to his decision, in 1929,
to "put a little showmanship in with the music."

Yet showmanship had been a part of Armstrong's
act since 1926, when he hammed it up for audiences
at the Sunset Cafe. What actually happened in the
1930s was that Armstrong beckoned to listeners in a
more intimate way than ever before. Hard times had
taught him to savor his moments onstage, for only
there could he salve the pain of racism, of botched
friendships and marriages, of the ruinous fates that
overtook old heroes.

As a person, Armstrong was as vulnerable as anyone else. As a performer, he rose to a lofty, protected height and took his listeners with him, gathering them in a tight embrace and comforting them with his humor, compassion, wisdom—and something else: an infectious joy that eludes description but that radiates from his recordings, his film (and, later, television) appearances, and even from candid photographs taken backstage or in moments of relaxation.

Joy had always been present in Armstrong's music. But the passing of his youth brought it closer to the surface. And just as he made a gift of joy to his listeners, so he felt indebted to them—complete strangers, different faces every night—for yielding to the magic of his gift and for letting him bask in the tender gaze of the spotlight. With stardom, Armstrong discovered, as he later put it, "the main thing is to live for that audience, live for the public." ✺

Once Armstrong became a star, he remained a headliner, outlasting almost every performer of his generation. One reason for his enduring success was his willingness to travel all across the country and play one-nighters, which kept him before the public. "I don't mind travelling," he said, "that's where the audiences are—in the towns and cities—and that's what I want, the audience."

8

AT THE TOP

❦

THROUGHOUT THE 1930s, Alpha Smith remained Armstrong's steady companion. She wanted to formalize their relationship by marriage, but he resisted—until 1938, when Alpha insisted he ask Lil for a divorce. Lil granted it, and Armstrong was wed for the third time.

It was Armstrong's briefest stab at matrimony. Despite all their years of easy intimacy, he and Alpha failed dismally as husband and wife. Alpha did not try to dominate Armstrong—his main gripe against Lil—but she irked him in other ways. Her "mind was on furs, diamonds, and other flashy luxuries," he said, "and not enough on me and my happiness." They were divorced in 1940.

The marriage was probably doomed in any case. Mere months after the ceremony, Armstrong fell for another woman: 24-year-old Lucille Wilson. A native New Yorker, Lucille was born to a middle-class family in the borough of Queens. As a child, she studied the piano and dance but did not aspire to enter show business. Then the depression bankrupted her father's taxicab company and forced her to put her training to practical use. She landed a job as a dancer at Harlem's Alhambra Theatre, appeared in a Broadway

The raspiness in Armstrong's singing voice—one of the traits for which he is best known—was due in part to growths on his vocal chords. In 1936, he sought to have these nodules removed, but the operation proved unsuccessful and the roughness in his voice remained.

Lucille Wilson in 1938, at about the time Armstrong first met her at the Cotton Club, where he had a six-month engagement. Four years later, after a stormy start to their relationship, she became his fourth wife.

chorus line, and moved on to steady work at the Cotton Club.

When Armstrong spotted Lucille there in 1938, he was instantly smitten. Although a freshly minted husband, he began wooing the young woman in earnest. Lucille was not in the market for a married man and kept her distance. But Armstrong would not give up. After his gig ended, he constantly phoned and wrote. A year later, he returned to New York, and the pair began a courtship that culminated in marriage in 1942.

Lucille proved the ideal spouse for Armstrong. She doted on him (as Daisy Parker and Alpha Smith had not), but did not overwhelm him (as Lil sometimes had). She succeeded, in short, in indulging her husband's whims without sacrificing her own independence. And she often divined her husband's needs better than he did himself—for instance, on the matter of housing. Long years on the road had turned Armstrong into a nomad, content to put up in hotels for months at a stretch. But Lucille preferred a stable home away from the hectic whirl of the music scene. Her husband objected, but finally yielded in 1946, allowing Lucille to pick out a modest two-story dwelling in Corona, the neighborhood where she had grown up. Armstrong grew so attached to the place that even after the area tumbled into decay he refused to move.

Offstage, Armstrong had found stability, but as a performer he could not relax. The music world was changing, and he labored to keep up. In the 1930s, Dixieland fell by the wayside, replaced by "swing," big-band music that owed much to the orchestral jazz pioneered by Fletcher Henderson in the 1920s. By 1935, this fetching blend of serious jazz and frothy dance music had become the rage among young listeners.

Armstrong was capable of playing swing. In fact, he had helped spawn its crisp rhythms, first with the

Fletcher Henderson Orchestra and then on the Hot
Five recordings. But he did not adjust smoothly to
the big-band format mastered by the best swing combos. Clarinetist Benny Goodman, trombonist Glenn
Miller, and others fronted groups whose instrument
sections meshed like the moving parts of a power-
driven motor. But even with the backing of a solid
ensemble such as the Luis Russell Orchestra, Armstrong remained a solo act. Instead of honing his
sidemen into a sleek unit, he corseted them in dull
and plodding arrangements.

His outmoded style cost Armstrong some younger
fans, but he remained a favorite with older listeners,
who bought his records, awaited his films, and tuned
in to his radio performances. In 1940, he was a big
enough attraction to make it back to Broadway as
one of the leads in *Swinging the Dream*, a musical
updating of Shakespeare's sprightly comedy, *A Mid-
summer Night's Dream*. Benny Goodman also appeared in the cast, as did Zutty Singleton. The show
flopped, but Armstrong's work was praised by the
critics.

Then, once again, the music world was overtaken
by larger events. On December 7, 1941, Japanese
bombers attacked the American naval base at Pearl
Harbor, Hawaii, plunging the United States into World
War II. The entire nation—including entertainers—
pitched in to the war effort. Armstrong made the
rounds of U.S. military bases, where he performed
for the troops; took to the airwaves on broadcasts
sponsored by Armed Forces Radio Services; and played
alongside other top jazzmen on a series of "victory"
disks issued by the government.

When hostilities ended in 1945, much of the
civilized world had been laid to waste. Battles fought
in Italy and France had left charming villages looking
like excavated ruins. Splendid capitals—London, Paris,
Berlin, and Moscow—gaped with charred buildings.
Two major Japanese cities, Hiroshima and Nagasaki,

had been flattened into rubble by a new American weapon: the atomic bomb.

An ocean away, the United States seemed fresh, healthy, and strong. Its sickly depression economy had been revived by the war effort, which put legions of unemployed men and women back to work. Militarily, the country had attained tremendous prestige as the leader of the Western alliance that defeated Nazi Germany and Japan.

America was far from a perfect place, however. It was, rather, two places, two countries. One had dismantled the anti-Semitic regime of Adolf Hitler; the other had expelled thousands of innocent Japanese-Americans from their homes and confined them to internment camps. One spent billions of dollars to help rebuild Europe; the other forced black servicemen into segregated regiments. Many black soldiers returned with harrowing tales of white officers who treated them less humanely than they did enemy prisoners captured in combat. America was split in two by the hard wedge of racism.

Two of jazz's most influential artists—Armstrong and Billie Holiday—teamed up in New Orleans, *a 1946 film that attempted to re-create Storyville in the early 1900s. Although the movie was a failure in many ways, it included several authentic touches, such as the early-model cornet played by Armstrong in this scene.*

Jim Crow had become a national shame, a deepening furrow in the American character. Enlightened citizens called for action. In 1946, President Harry S. Truman appointed a committee, composed of prominent whites and blacks, that issued a report harshly critical of racial discrimination. Truman's administration then adopted a policy of redressing centuries of injustice. It abolished segregation in the armed forces, funded "open" housing projects, and urged employers to hire more black workers.

As blacks edged closer to social acceptance, Armstrong's following widened. One event made the difference. In 1946, a Hollywood movie company, the Hal Roach Studios, announced plans for a musical extravaganza, *New Orleans*, about the birth of jazz. Some 30 years had passed since the strains of the new music first filtered past the boundaries of Storyville. Dixieland had since become passé among some listeners, but others prized it as a staple of American culture. A nostalgic haze now enveloped the gritty environment that had nurtured Armstrong and others—the honky-tonks, the brothels, the cutting contests. A Dixieland revival had even taken root, and old stars such as Kid Ory found new life playing vintage New Orleans tunes.

Filming for *New Orleans* was scheduled to begin in 1947. But musical preparations got under way sooner. In the summer of 1946, Armstrong and several other Storyville veterans—including Kid Ory, Zutty Singleton, and clarinetist Barney Bigard—gathered in a Hollywood music studio to lay down a sound track. In the fall, the group—with another drummer sitting in for Singleton—rerecorded songs from the film for release as an album.

Armstrong's talent for spontaneity—always a key to his popularity—impressed the filmmakers who created *New Orleans*. Whereas even a star improviser such as Billie Holiday was instructed to follow the script to the letter, Armstrong was given free reign. Bigard, who was on the set, remembered that the director "let [Armstrong] have his head as to the personality he played. . . . He could say anything and get away with it . . . Everyone knows about his greatness as an artist, but as an individual, a character, nobody could touch him."

While he was in Hollywood, Armstrong received a visit from Leonard Feather, a pianist, songwriter, and jazz critic. Feather had been recruited by Delaunay, a French record label, to sign up the star for a recording session with a small ensemble instead of the big bands Armstrong customarily fronted. When Armstrong agreed to make the record, Feather advised him to take the experiment further and appear onstage with a small group.

Critics and fans had been pushing for this change since the early 1930s, but Armstrong had grown comfortable with the big-band format and was reluctant to shift gears. So was Joe Glaser, who judged small bands to be box-office poison. Feather was relentless, however, and at last Armstrong agreed to a compromise. He would do as Feather wished, but only on the condition that he play two sets: one with a small group, the other with his big band.

On February 8, 1947, Carnegie Hall in New York City buzzed with expectant fans. For the first time in nearly two decades, Armstrong took the stage with a small combo, members of a group that had been gigging locally. As Feather predicted, the show was a smash. In fact, Armstrong summarily dismissed his big band—except for drummer "Big" Sid Catlett, who was joined by a select group of Dixieland aces at a second concert, this time at Town Hall, another major New York spot.

These concerts—and Armstrong's refurbished identity as a jazz player—generated so much publicity that Glaser decided to capitalize on the new format. The manager contacted some of the best-known players of Armstrong's generation—trombonist Jack Teagarden, Earl Hines (who had been leading his own big band), Bigard, and Catlett—and proposed that they tour with his client. Glaser dubbed the group Louis Armstrong and the All Stars and booked them into a Los Angeles nightclub in August 1947. The press built up the event, celebrities turned out en masse, and soon Armstrong was on top again, heading the highest-paid jazz group in America. He continued to play with the All Stars through the 1960s, despite many changes in personnel.

The return to the small-band format added luster to Armstrong's reputation. So did the premiere of *New Orleans* on June 9, 1947, though the movie paled in comparison to the concerts. Instead of providing an authentic glimpse of jazz and its origins, *New Orleans* turned out to be a silly love story starring Bing Crosby, the popular white crooner. Still, it thrust Armstrong further into public view.

Onstage, Armstrong had switched to the format that best suited his unique artistry, but he continued to present himself as an all-purpose showman. He reprised hits—his own and others—rather than test

Armstrong poses with several members of the All Stars, whose personnel—(from left to right) pianist Earl Hines, trombonist Jack Teagarden, drummer Cozy Cole, clarinetist Barney Bigard, and bassist Arvell Shaw—included some of the jazz giants of his generation. The band, which was formed in 1947, remained together for 17 years.

out new material. And he made a conscious effort to distance himself from the latest development in jazz, "bebop," which sprouted up in jazz clubs that lined 52nd Street in New York City. At one such place, Minton's, the new style received its christening from an exasperated Fats Waller, who complained to a roomful of musicians during one jam session in the early 1940s, "Stop that crazy boppin' and a-stoppin' and play . . . like the rest of us guys."

The inventors of bebop—especially saxophonist Charlie "Bird" Parker and trumpeter Dizzy Gillespie—propelled jazz in a dramatically new direction. To them, jazz was not dance music but art of the highest order, on a par with the compositions of the European classical tradition. They scorned catchy melodies, bouncy rhythms, and zesty arrangements in favor of bold experimentation. These new players did not merely bend the rules—they snapped them. The result contrasted as starkly with standard jazz as a cubist portrait contrasts with the Mona Lisa. Bebop disturbed more listeners than it pleased—one Los Angeles radio station banned it from the airwaves—but it changed jazz forever.

As radical as bebop was, it could not have come into being without Armstrong's groundbreaking work

The nature of jazz changed dramatically after World War II as a result of the innovations of bebop musicians such as saxophonist Charlie "Bird" Parker and trumpeter Dizzy Gillespie. The duo is shown here performing at Birdland, a New York City club named for Parker.

as a solo improviser. Younger artists went him one better, however. Instead of treating melodies as the springboard for highly tuneful inventions, Parker and Gillespie used them as launching pads for exotic solo flights that included shrieks, squeals, and barks. They also wrought havoc with standard tempos. "Them cats play all the wrong notes," Armstrong said, in what became an oft-quoted remark.

A much different issue also pitted Armstrong against the new wave. Bebop artists often struck a combative pose toward audiences, critics, and, especially, older musicians, whom they accused of pandering to the white crowd. Armstrong came under severe attack, not so much for his playing as for his manner—his habit of taking the stage wearing a huge grin that stayed plastered on his face for the duration of his act. He seemed too eager to play the shuffling, obliging black.

This criticism stung Armstrong, but it did not change his resolve to "live for that audience." In 1949, he accepted an invitation to return to his hometown as a participant in Mardi Gras. This annual event, still the best-known feature of New Orleans life, has its origins in the Roman Catholic tradition of Lent, a time of penitence that begins seven weeks before Easter. In New Orleans, the occasion is heralded by a citywide, open-air binge. On the final day of the festivities (Shrove Tuesday, or, in French, Mardi Gras), motorized floats topped by costumed celebrants roll down the city's main thoroughfares, witnessed by thousands of spectators.

Each year, Mardi Gras is planned by the city's network of elite social clubs. Today, many blacks participate, but in the 1940s only one black social club, called the Zulus, had a role in the pageant, nominating a local black man to be "King of the Zulus." It was a great honor for the chosen one, who donned an elaborate costume, smothered his face with

Armstrong, dressed as king of the Zulus, rides on a float during the 1949 Mardi Gras festival in New Orleans. His appearance in this antic role upset jazz purists as well as black leaders, who felt that making such a foolish spectacle was not appropriate behavior for a role model like Armstrong.

makeup, and mounted a float alongside his queen—a local black woman selected by the club. Then, as their float rolled through the streets, the couple tossed coconuts to the massed onlookers.

In 1949, the Zulus broke with precedent and looked outside the local community for a king. They elected the most illustrious of all black New Orleans men, Louis Armstrong, who had deserted the city a quarter century before. Armstrong gladly accepted the invitation. His homecoming caused headlines. *Time* magazine put him on its cover, and photos of him in his Zulu garb appeared in newspapers around the country. But outside New Orleans, some blacks objected to Armstrong's performance and denounced him as a minstrel, debasing himself for the amusement of southern whites.

In the 1950s, Armstrong's tours with the All Stars elevated him to such renown that it blunted the criticism of the Young Turks of the jazz scene and of civil rights leaders. Yet, on a few occasions he surprised both groups with his outspokenness, most memorably when the southern city of Little Rock, Arkansas, refused in 1957 to comply with the Supreme Court's decision in the case of *Brown v. the Board of Education.* The court's ruling, handed down in 1954, declared that it was illegal for the nation's public schools to be segregated; three years later, nine black students were admitted to a white high school in Little Rock. The fierce opposition of the local whites and of Arkansas governor Orville Faubus caused a nationwide furor as the first day of school approached.

On September 18, 1957, Armstrong was booked to perform in Grand Forks, North Dakota. A local newspaperman who stopped by Armstrong's dressing room for an interview found the star with his eyes glued to a television news report. It showed a black teenager, who had been denied entrance to Little

Rock's Central High, encircled by a howling mob of angry whites. Armstrong was disgusted by their actions and said so, pulling no punches. He accused President Dwight D. Eisenhower, who had not yet interceded on behalf of blacks, of having "no guts" and said the U.S. government could "go to hell." The reporter wrote down every word, and Armstrong's remarks appeared in newspapers around the country.

On subsequent occasions, Armstrong made equally pointed comments, but by and large he sidestepped this heated topic. Some critics interpreted his caution as cowardice, an unwillingness to take a stand that might damage his popularity. The charge was not completely unfounded. His primary mission, at least since the late 1920s, had been to please his fans.

But Armstrong's detractors failed to see that his seeming indifference to the civil rights struggle was of a piece with his refusal to let others—black or white—dictate his actions. His first loyalty was to his audience, and nothing would stop him from honoring the pact he had made with them decades before, when they had singled him out for stardom by purchasing his records and lining up for his gigs. And, despite his cheery manner onstage, he brimmed with commentary about the unique frustrations felt by black Americans. His pained blues vocals and defiant trumpet solos sprang from the same well of suffering that prompted other blacks to call for social reform.

Had Armstrong tailored his performances to ideological fashion, he would have betrayed his own gifts. In the end, even the bebop artists came to understand this. Dizzy Gillespie, who at first deeply resented Armstrong's clowning style, later said, "What I had considered [Armstrong's] grinning in the face of racism [was actually] his absolute refusal to let anything, even anger about racism, steal the joy from his life." ❀

Surrounded by a crowd of taunting whites, Elizabeth Eckford tries to enter Central High School in Little Rock, Arkansas. Shortly after Armstrong and many other Americans voiced their disgust over the 1957 incident, President Dwight D. Eisenhower ordered 1,000 paratroopers as well as the National Guard to clear the way for black students so they could enter the school.

9

"SATCHMO
THE GREAT"

POLITICS, STRANGELY ENOUGH, shaped the final triumphant chapter of Louis Armstrong's career, which saw him emerge in the late 1950s as one of the best-known people in the world. Since the 1930s, he had been amassing an audience that crossed the borders not only of race but also of nations. His first trip abroad, in 1932, had been a success. His second had blossomed into a lengthy stay that took him all over Europe. During the 1940s and 1950s, the touring schedule of the All Stars included numerous overseas dates. So popular was Armstrong outside the United States that in 1960 the State Department enlisted him to make a series of long-distance tours meant to improve international relations.

Armstrong's visits—especially those to Asia and Africa—generated enormous publicity back home. Almost every day, it seemed, news of his latest stop-over appeared in the papers and on television. Americans grew used to seeing him encircled by foreign dignitaries, posing with exotic instruments, or mopping his brow with a handkerchief. The grand old man of jazz—nicknamed "Pops" by younger players—had become a living symbol of American high spirits.

His eminence had been formally acknowledged as early as 1957, when a television program, "Salute to Satch," aired nationwide. It was an assemblage of Armstrong footage put together by Edward R. Mur-

Armstrong giving a performance at the age of 50, in a typical pose: alone at the mike, with handkerchief and trumpet in hand.

With his wife Lucille looking on, Armstrong serenades an Egyptian sphinx in 1961. His visit to the Middle East was part of his international tour as goodwill ambassador for the U.S. State Department.

row, the noted television newsman. The star himself narrated in his husky, intimate voice. Later, the program was expanded into a film, *Satchmo the Great*. At the same time, Decca released a special four-record set that encapsulated Armstrong's long career, from his days with the Creole Jazz Band through the 1950s. He also recorded two new hits: "Mack the Knife" (from the musical *Threepenny Opera*) and the ballad "Blueberry Hill."

Armstrong even reached a new audience. In 1963, the producers of the Broadway musical *Hello, Dolly!* wanted to promote the show by having its title tune recorded by a big-name vocalist. Through Joe Glaser, they arranged a date with Armstrong, and a couple of months later, "Hello, Dolly!" was released as a single. It climbed steadily up the *Billboard* chart, and on May 9, 1964, it reached number one—the first Armstrong song ever to occupy the top slot—dethroning the Beatles' "Can't Buy Me Love."

On the heels of this success came an album of Armstrong classics, featuring Louis Armstrong and the All Stars. It, too, topped *Billboard*'s chart, on June 13, 1964. Some 50 years after leaving the Colored Waifs' Home and 40 years after leaving New Orleans, Armstrong had emerged as the best-selling pop star in the nation.

In a profession where even great stars quickly fade into obscurity, Armstrong's fame not only endured but enlarged. Why? One clue has been provided by Barney Bigard, who grew up in New Orleans when Armstrong did, shared the stage with him in Chicago and New York, and spent hundreds of hours in his company—onstage and off—with the All Stars. A jazz master himself, Bigard realized that Armstrong had a quality none of his peers possessed. The clarinetist stated, "Louis was exactly the same on stage as off stage. Exactly. There never was any hidden side to him. You bought what you saw with him. He came 'as is.'"

Naturalness was just as essential to Armstrong's art as was his technical mastery. Indeed, it crucially aided his musical gifts. Naturalness enabled him to improvise riskily, to touch his listeners directly, to unburden himself on stage without fear of embarrassment, and, ultimately, to attain a special category among 20th-century artists. It made him not only popular but—a much rarer thing—beloved.

Yet the star himself scarcely acknowledged the privileged status he had attained. In fact, he lived in perpetual fear of losing his fans. Thus, even when his health was in danger, he refused to slow his frantic pace. For most of his life, Armstrong had avoided serious medical problems. His scarred lip hampered his playing, but it was far from a life-threatening ailment. The same was true of other maladies that cropped up in his later years: a mild case of diabetes, recurrent bronchitis, and, beginning in the 1940s, ulcer attacks.

In 1969, six years after recording the title song of Hello, Dolly! to help publicize the Broadway musical, Armstrong appeared with singer and actress Barbra Streisand (who was also managed by Joe Glaser) in the screen version of the show.

Armstrong limbers up in his backstage dressing room before a concert. Always eager to perform, he continued at a hectic pace even after his doctors urged him to retire.

In the next decade, however, Armstrong's health began to deteriorate. The warning signal came in 1959, in Spoleto, Italy, where Armstrong participated in an international jazz festival. One night, his companions found him writhing on the floor near the bed in his hotel room. He had suffered a major heart attack. Luckily, his entourage included a physician, Dr. Alexander Schiff, who comforted the stricken star and then rushed him to a nearby hospital.

Under Schiff's supervision, Armstrong recuperated amid heaps of get-well cards sent from all over the world. He could not bear confinement, however. After only a week, he rose from his sickbed and sped off to Rome, where he sang until dawn in a nightclub. Days later, he flew back to the United States and made a surprise appearance at an open-air jazz extravaganza.

During Armstrong's last years, top-notch doctors hovered over him, yet he preferred homegrown treatments—"crazy remedies," as he termed them. Most of them came from his mother, who placed great stock in Creole lore. Sounder remedies were urged on Armstrong by Gary Zucker, a New York physician who specialized in heart disease. He told the star to banish salt from his diet, to lose weight, and to lighten his schedule. Armstrong only half listened—until 1968, when heart failure affected the functioning of his kidneys, causing his body to swell up with so much fluid that he could not squeeze into his shoes. Thereafter, he made a much greater effort to obey Zucker's advice.

Armstrong's decline continued, however. In 1969, his heart and kidney troubles multiplied, forcing him to spend three months in New York's Beth Israel Hospital. Joe Glaser, on his way to the hospital to visit his prize client, suffered a stroke, then lapsed into a coma, from which he never recovered. He died on June 4, 1969. Armstrong was devastated. His relationship with Glaser had been strictly professional, but it had spanned 30 triumphant years.

Since first signing Armstrong in 1935, Glaser had built a large management empire. At various times, his clients had included some of the top singing stars in the country: Billie Holiday, Ella Fitzgerald, Pearl Bailey, and Barbra Streisand. Thus, Glaser left a large estate. All his shares in International Music, a sheet-music publisher, went to Armstrong, as did handsome compensation for the income Glaser had been "holding" for three decades.

Armstrong did not need the money. The All Star tours had filled his bank account nicely, as had his appearances in big-budget films such as *High Society* (released in 1956). In addition, he had modest tastes. On his travels, he was feted so lavishly that he preferred simple pleasures when he returned home.

In his sixties, Armstrong frequently visited Harlem, where he palled with fans and doled out cash—as much as $500 a night—to acquaintances down on their luck. Another choice haunt was Shea Stadium, in Flushing, Queens, where he rooted for the New York Mets from a box seat. And he spent many hours on his front stoop surrounded by neighborhood children—substitutes, perhaps, for the children he never had.

But these comforts could not quench Armstrong's thirst for applause. He constantly appeared onstage and on television, though bronchitis rendered him useless on the trumpet and made singing painful. He had nothing left to prove, but he could not stop performing.

By 1971, Armstrong was near death, yet he insisted on more gigs, including a two-week engagement at New York's Waldorf Astoria Hotel. "I've got bookings arranged and the people are waiting for me," he told Gary Zucker. "I got to do it, Doc. I got to do it."

With the help of a youngster, an aged Armstrong walks his dog—a gift from Joe Glaser—near his home in Corona, Queens. Throughout his life, the star performer remained approachable to young and old alike.

This gig was his last. After he finished it, he returned to Beth Israel. He was released on May 5, and exactly two months later—on July 5—he planned to start rehearsing for another tour with the All Stars. The next morning—July 6, 1971—Louis Armstrong died of kidney failure.

The news rippled across the world. President Richard M. Nixon hailed Armstrong as "one of the architects of an American art form, a free and individual spirit, and an artist of worldwide fame." Nixon arranged for Armstrong's body to lie in state at the National Guard Armory at 66th Street and Park Avenue in New York City, where 25,000 mourners paid their respects.

Armstrong was dead but not silenced. Today, he remains a force in popular music. In 1988, he climbed up the charts with his recording of "What a Wonderful World," part of the soundtrack to the hit film *Good Morning, Vietnam*, starring comedian Robin Williams. And "Do You Know What It Means to Miss New Orleans?," the theme song of *New Orleans*, resurfaced weekly on the television comedy series "Frank's Place."

Even more significant is the imprint that Armstrong left on 20th-century music. His solo flights opened up vistas that later jazz artists continue to explore. His rough-hewn vocal style remains the model for many popular singers.

Outside the world of music, Armstrong's remarkable career resonates with meaning. His odyssey touched crucial bases of 20th-century black experience: New Orleans, where a great art form was born; Chicago, the "top of the world" for a generation of migrants who threw off the shackles of the Deep South; New York City, the seat of the Harlem Renaissance; Europe, a haven free of the racism that tainted daily life in America; and Africa, where the story of black America began three centuries ago.

Talent enabled Armstrong to go far, but the ride was never smooth. At every way station, he faced the risks, anxieties, and pressures faced by nearly every black American of his time. Armstrong's grandest triumph, perhaps, was staring down his own doubts. Reared in the suffocating cradle of Jim Crow, he dared to aspire to fame. Initially shy of the spotlight, he became the outstanding showman of his era.

Armstrong did not merely rise to each new challenge, he soared above it. His colleague Barney Bigard wrote that "nobody was bigger than Louis." He could have written that Armstrong was somehow larger than himself. Jazz, the form he helped invent, has been enshrined among the permanent glories of our culture. And Louis Armstrong's musical genius still transports listeners into cloudless realms of unbridled joy. ◖◗

SELECTED DISCOGRAPHY

————— ◖◗ —————

The sounds of Louis Armstrong have been captured on many different recordings. The following albums, which highlight important phases of his career as a trumpeter and vocalist, offer a good introduction to his music: *The Best of Louis Armstrong* (MCA Records), *Ella & Louis* (MGM Records), *The Genius of Louis Armstrong* (Columbia Records), *Louis Armstrong* (RCA Victor), *Louis Armstrong and King Oliver* (Milestone Records), *Louis Armstrong and the Hot Five* (Columbia Records), and *Louis Armstrong's Greatest Hits* (Columbia Records).

CHRONOLOGY

————— ◖◗ —————

c. 1899	Born Louis Armstrong in New Orleans, Louisiana
c. 1912	Sent to Colored Waifs' Home; learns to play the cornet
c. 1914	Begins professional career in Storyville
1916	Meets Joe Oliver
1917	Replaces Oliver in Kid Ory's Orchestra
1918	Marries Daisy Parker
1919	Joins Fate Marable's dance orchestra on a Mississippi riverboat
1922	Joins Oliver's Creole Jazz Band in Chicago
1924	Marries Lillian Hardin; joins the Fletcher Henderson Orchestra in New York City
1925	Makes first Hot Five recordings
1928	Records "West End Blues" on June 26
1929	Stars on Broadway in *Hot Chocolates*; switches to big-band format
1931	First European tour
1935	Signs management contract with Joe Glaser
1938	Marries Alpha Smith
1942	Marries Lucille Wilson; moves to Corona, New York
1947	Forms Louis Armstrong and His All Stars
1960	Becomes goodwill ambassador for the U.S. State Department
1964	"Hello, Dolly!" becomes the nation's number-one record
1971	Armstrong dies in Corona, New York, on July 6

FURTHER READING

Armstrong, Louis. *Satchmo: My Life in New Orleans.* New York: Da Capo Press, 1986.

Bigard, Barney. *With Louis and the Duke: The Autobiography of a Jazz Clarinetist.* New York: Oxford University Press, 1986.

Buerkle Jack V., and Danny Barker. *Bourbon Street Black: The New Orleans Black Jazzmen.* New York: Oxford University Press, 1973.

Clayton, Buck. *Buck Clayton's Jazz World.* New York: Oxford University Press, 1987.

Collier, James Lincoln. *Louis Armstrong: An American Genius.* New York: Oxford University Press, 1983.

Gourse, Leslie. *Louis' Children: American Jazz Singers.* New York: Morrow, 1984.

Meryman, Richard. *Louis Armstrong: A Self-Portrait: The Interview by Richard Meryman.* New York: The Eakins Press, 1966, 1971.

Rose, Al. *Storyville, New Orleans.* Tuscaloosa: University of Alabama Press, 1974.

Shapiro, Nat, and Nat Hentoff: *Hear Me Talkin' To Ya: The Story of Jazz as Told by the Men Who Made It.* New York: Dover, 1966.

Shaw, Arnold. *The Jazz Age: Popular Music in the 1920's.* New York: Oxford University Press, 1987.

Stearns, Marshall. *The Story of Jazz.* New York: Oxford University Press, 1956.

INDEX

SAM TANENHAUS holds degrees in literature from Grinnell College and Yale University. He is the author of *Literature Unbound: A Guide for the Common Reader* and "Italo Calvino" (in *European Writers: The Twentieth Century*, edited by George Stade). His book reviews have appeared in the *New York Times Book Review*, *Village Voice*, *Chicago Tribune*, and *Chicago Sun-Times*. He was a Junior Fellow at the New York Institute for the Humanities in 1983–84 and has taught English at Baruch College. He lives in New York City, where he works as an editor.

NATHAN IRVIN HUGGINS is W.E.B. Du Bois Professor of History and Director of the W.E.B. Du Bois Institute for Afro-American Research at Harvard University. He previously taught at Columbia University. Professor Huggins is the author of numerous books, including *Black Odyssey: The Afro-American Ordeal in Slavery*, *The Harlem Renaissance*, and *Slave and Citizen: The Life of Frederick Douglass*.

PICTURE CREDITS